Mosaic
Taking the Pieces of Your Life and Creating A Masterpiece!

Martina A. Alford

Copyright © 2018 by Martina A. Alford

All rights reserved. No portion of this book may be reproduced mechanically, electronically, or by any other means, including photocopying, without written permission of the publisher. It is illegal to copy this book, post it on a website or distribute it by any other means without permission from the publisher.

Martina A. Alford/ 4P Publishing
Chattanooga, TN 37421
lonlyknowonesong@gmail.com

Editor: Shavonna Bush

Contributing Editors: Alisha M. Alford, Tarina Whiteside

Cover/designer: LINZI WANN LLC

Photographer: Chauncey D. Alford

Limits of Liability and Disclaimer of Warranty

The author and publisher shall not be liable for your misuse of this material. This book is strictly for informational and educational purposes. The purpose of this book is to inspire. The author and publisher do not guarantee anyone following these techniques, suggestions, tips, ideas, or strategies will become successful. This book is not intended as a substitute for best judgement or the medical advice of professionals.

The author and publisher shall have neither liability nor responsibility to anyone with respect to any loss or damage caused or alleged to be caused, directly or indirectly by the information contained in this book.

Book Layout © 2016 BookDesignTemplates.com

Mosaic/ Martina A. Alford. -- 1st Ed.
ISBN 978-1-941749-80-7

Library of Congress Control Number: 2018908426

Dedication

Thank You, God, for choosing me and operating within me. You've given me life, strength, and victory. You've been my light in the darkness, my compass through it all. Your love is unquestionable, and you give me peace.

Thank you, Donald Boddie Jr., for always believing in me, motivating me and challenging me, for holding me accountable and encouraging me to be my truest self. Thank you for taking out the time to care for me when I needed you and thank you for your input on this book! You've always had high expectations of me, and I cannot recall one time over the decades that you didn't believe in me. I appreciate you!

To my Children: Chauncey, Amon, Tarina, I encourage you to SLOW DOWN, always put God first, know yourself, discover your purpose, respect wisdom and continue to grow. It is through you, I have learned my greatest lessons of unconditional love, perseverance, motivation, patience, and faith and it is for you that I strive to leave a beautiful legacy.

To my mother, Gwendolyn Ewing, the older I get, the more I understand, and respect who you are. You've shown me that the key to a peaceful life is to just decide what makes you happy and unapologetically pursue it. To my father, Donald L Alford, Sr., many of the things you tried to teach us in our youth, I now understand and value. Because of you, I am "loading my wagon and shaking my line."

Thank you to my sister Alisha M. Alford, for the conversations and the late-night reading. I admire your attention to detail and your way with words. Thank you to my brother Steven E. Alford, who is also my friend. You and I have always been connected in ways stronger than that of siblings. You have admirable wisdom and strength! You've always had a demeanor opposite my fiery one and you speak to me in divine ways. You have been my confidant, my helper, my buddy, my advisor! You know everything about me and have always purely accepted me as I am. I thank you for your encouragement and I just thank you for being you.

Thank you to my aunt Barbara Ewing. You've dried many tears, listened to many stories and came to my rescue many times. We've laughed, we've cried, and we've discovered together. I admire your wisdom and aspire to be as graceful as you. I am grateful that we were divinely paired to run this race.

To my longtime friend LaKeisha Banks, who knows and has seen many things I've gone through, yet you're still hanging around. You constantly remind me to take my own advice and you remind me that there are people in my circle rooting for me.

To my godmother Melgie Smith, from the moment we met, we just clicked and you are one that has shown me unconditional love and non-judgment. You are purely yourself with me and allow me to be the same with you. When you took me under your wing, you showed me that God places people in our lives when we need them and assured me that you are here to stay. I get happy at the thought of you and am so happy that you chose me!

To my Mentors: Laura Brown and Shavonna Bush, thank you for pushing me out of my comfort zone, for the motivation, guidance, structure, and advice.

In memory of cousin Martice D. Moore, you continue to guide me and inspire me to "Do you cuzzo." You are the inspiration behind "OneSong" ministry. "I only know one song but I'll sing it for you".

In memory of Grandad George Ewing who had the most beautiful flower garden on the block. In the midst of a chaotic city, taught me love and peace. In memory of Grandma Lucille Ewing who taught me how taking care of home and the people in it are a priority over everything else.

In Memory of Granddaddy Eddie Alford Sr. who taught me to find humor in every day. In memory of Grandmama Sadie Alford, who taught me to trust, smile, pray, have faith in God and always keep a song in your heart.

This is always the difficult part because there are so many people who have guided and encouraged me along the way. The wisdom and guidance I have attained, I owe to the many unnamed people who have encouraged me to press on, I thank you. To the people who have challenged me, I thank you. To those seasonally by my side, I thank you for your time. To those who have remained by my side, I appreciate you.

CONTENTS

Preface	9
Introduction	11
Mind	15
Purge	17
Baggage	21
Self Esteem	23
Self-Control	25
Conflict	27
Freedom	31
Motivation	33
Image	37
Style	39
Character	41
Health	43
Soul	47
Unapologetic	49
Power	51
Cultivate	53
Love	57
Trust	59
Peace	63
Patience	65
Growth	67
Communication	71
Limitations and Boundaries	75
Responsibility	79
Accountability	83
Family	85
Friends	89
Pride	93
Society and Acceptance	97
Environment	101
Decisions	103
Perseverance	105
Time	107
Just Like That	109

Preface

So here we are, at the point of adulthood, expecting to be great. It's like, as soon as we crossed that esteemed age, life stepped in and said, "Hey, you're an adult now, go live," but we have no clue what that means. So we wake up each day and do our best to figure it out.

We observe the world around us. We try to understand what's expected, how to accomplish things, what paths to take and how to play the cards we are dealt. When good moments come, we celebrate, and when bad moments happen, we detach. Life is a journey full of ups and downs so how do we deal with that?

I've learned that you have to be intentional. You have to make a conscious decision to live your life, rather than just running the clock, getting through each day. It's like a game. Already laid out before you are paths full of advances and obstacles. You have a certain amount of resources, some you choose and some you are given, and you must walk your own path using what you have, being who you are.

Your journey is individual, although alongside others. That means, although there are people who will go through life with you, there are some things you must do and learn on your own. Life is lived using part strategy (wisdom) and part roll of the dice (destiny, things we cannot control). You can't be too arrogant because life is to be enjoyed, nor get too frustrated because there are still cards left in the deck. No matter how long it takes, no matter how many obstacles you face, no matter how many other players are in the game, you focus on your journey, with a goal to win.

Life has no manual. There is no secret key and no special code. Not everything works for everyone. No two paths are the same. Life is a journey, and what makes it fulfilling is the ability to take all the knowledge, experience, trials, triumphs, everything that happened to you, all of your dreams and walk your path, run your race, enjoying your life along the way!

Introduction

We were a close-knit family. I'm the second oldest, first daughter of 5. Growing up, our lives consisted of school, church, family and playing with neighborhood children. Most of the houses on our street were single family homes with yards, two parents with multiple children. I don't think we even knew what an apartment was and we had no clue what a blended family was.

Mama was from the city and dad from the country, and although we were raised in a suburban environment, we were well rounded. We had a large extended family and spent time with both sides

The five of us were stair steps, between one and one and a half years apart. Being so close in age, we did almost everything together, and we shared essentially everything, including unspoken secrets of the soul.

Life started to change once I reached middle school and our parents separated. The children were split between both parents and taken to two different states, many miles apart. This was very different for us because we usually traveled as a group. When one went, we all went.

Although it affected us in ways we have yet to fully understand, we never talked about the separation. We just accepted it as just something that happened. Adjusting to family change, dealing with childhood secrets, moving to a new environment, and experiencing adolescence wasn't easy, but we had to adjust to our new lives, so we did the best way we knew how.

I was one of those who moved with my mother to the city where the population was higher, everything moved faster, and life was just different. But, things didn't work out well, so I moved back in with my father. After completing a year of high school there, he allowed me to move in with his sister so I could be around more female influence.

That was fun at first. She taught me many things, but that was short-lived, so I ended up moving out on my own.

By the time I was seventeen, I lived about a hundred miles away from my closest parent. I had my own apartment, was working full time and finishing high school. I began to learn things on my own and became very independent. I finished high school with a certification as a nurse's assistant and provided patient care for a short while.

After graduating high school, I moved south, towards my mother and her family and a few months later, I became a mother. I went on to put myself through college, and while working towards my degree, became a mother again. I took pride in managing things for myself and my children.

After graduating from college as an Electronics and Computer Technician, I moved to Tennessee. I was again hundreds of miles away from any family. I knew no one there and had very little. As a matter of fact, all I had was the promise of a job, a station wagon, white with wood grain paneling, and a red leather third-row seat that faced backward, and our clothes. I had nowhere to stay. I left my sons with my mother for the summer and stayed in a hotel while I worked. I saved money so we could move into a new place by the time school began.

My two sons and I managed. We slowly progressed, eventually met many people and became more social. In this new town, we created a life for ourselves, and people started to know our names! Then I got married and soon after, gave birth to my daughter.

At the age of 30, I was a wife, mother, and step-mother. My career was progressing; I was managing a household, team mom for children's activities, active in church and a community volunteer. I was involved in many things and had what appeared to be a wonderful life. However, it was an illusion. My marriage was dysfunctional, which caused frustration, anxiety attacks, stress, depression and eventually, divorce. I was drained, distracted and detached. I felt as if I was walking in a constant state of numbness.

By my 40th birthday, I was so stressed out and was suffering mentally, physically and emotionally. I had to figure out how to recover, and found myself once again, independent. Everything in my life changed; my family, friends, finances, church, work, home, my body, my entire life was different. Then, shortly after my divorce was final, I ended up unexpectedly having double surgery.

As I laid recovering, I took the time to evaluate my life and I realized I was not where I wanted to be and this was not the life for me! I had to figure out how to get ahold of things and how to make my life the way I had envisioned. I began to ask myself, *"What do I do with the cards I've been dealt? How do I take control?"*

This was a wonderful opportunity for me to start writing my book. It came at a time after I experienced loss and darkness but was on my pathway to healing and progress. Most importantly, it came at a time when I was just plain old tired! I was tired of life as I knew it, tired of looking one way but feeling the other, tired of incompleteness, and tired of dysfunction! I always tell my children, *"When you are really tired of something, you WILL MAKE a change",* so that's what I decided to do.

I've always known there was a book inside of me. I have a story to tell. I just wasn't sure anyone wanted to hear. But time after time people would always ask me how I gained independence at such an early age. They would question how I was able to manage so many hats and conquer so many obstacles. They would constantly ask me the question "how". So, I began blogging and doing spoken word. I started sharing my story.

This is not a book about my struggle. Instead, it is to help us recognize we can be as successful and peaceful as we are created to be, even in the midst of trials and setbacks, second chances and re-plans. We must look within, gather the strength to overcome and build every aspect of our lives from the ground up on a solid foundation. We must take everything we have been through and everything we have been dealt and do something with it, make something from it!

In the words of my love, my supporter, my encourager, my realist, Donald Boddie, Jr., "*Tina, you need to get out of your own way*". I've learned to forgive so I can be free. I've learned to let go of some negative behaviors and adopt some excellent ones. I've learned that we have control over ourselves and our future. I've learned we have power; the power to start, power to stop, power to live, power to love, and the power to begin again.

Mosaic is an artistically crafted expression using pieces, intentionally arranged to create something beautiful. I want to encourage you to take all of the pieces of your life and intentionally create your own masterpiece! Each chapter in this book are areas within myself that I've identified that needed piecing together and I want to share that with you.

CHAPTER ONE

Mind

We live in a world of constant stimulation. It seems that there is always something going on with or around us. Whether it's someone telling us how to think, or giving us information to retain, there's always some kind of competition for our attention. Before you are ready to receive the things in store for you, you must first prepare yourself, starting with your mind. Question is: *How do I control my mind?*

Learning to control my mind has been a challenge. Besides the list of things that occupy my thought, at times, I also battle insecurities.

These insecurities make me revert back to that of a self-conscious child that felt like I was never smart enough or pretty enough, not strong enough, or social enough, just not good enough. I used to hold on to negative interactions and disappointments and somehow convince myself that these gloomy encounters dictate my path, and set the tone for my life. And my life reflected that. It looked great on the outside but inside, it was a mess.

Then came the day that I asked *myself, "What do YOU say about yourself? What do you see WITHIN yourself? What does GOD say about you?* Whatever you feel you deserve, you will accept, and whatever you believe, you will become. I refuse to believe that I'm destined to be that scared little inadequate girl for the rest of my life. So now when negative thoughts arise, I have to purposely encourage myself, and remind myself that my journey begins within. Even though difficult times and trials will come, if I master my mind, those times are more manageable.

I've searched for answers by reading, meditating, asking for guidance, and praying. Although those are excellent resources, I have discovered the key lies within me. Some of the things I needed for growth required understanding myself, learning what to hold on to, and letting go of the thoughts, habits, and conditioning that worked against me. I needed to strengthen my self-esteem, practice self-control, learn how to handle conflict, and I needed to find and keep myself motivated.

These next few chapters will address those things.

CHAPTER TWO

Purge

Purge: Cleanse, clear, purify, wash, remove, release, and let go. I've had to evaluate the things, people, places, habits, traditions, thoughts, and fears in my life and decide what I needed to keep and what I needed to let go.

I've had to let go of stuff. I call it stuff because it seems like we really want it when we get it but it eventually loses its value and becomes disposable, just another item in our space. Sometimes I can have bags full of trash and things to donate, yet still have a lot more stuff in my house! I don't understand how I can have so much stuff, and even after I get rid of a lot of stuff, still have so much stuff left!

Most times I'm looking at the item like, I remember when I bought this but never used it. Or, why did I buy SO MANY of these? Some are even the things that I have been holding on to that I once needed but no longer, or things that I've held onto for other people that weren't even mine! I've learned to keep only what I need for the time that I need, then let it go.

When I purge people, I consider my relationship with them and decide who's a friend, who's an acquaintance, whose temporary that I'm accepting as permanent, and who I only acquired through a mutual connection. I had to ask myself is this person adding to me, or subtracting from me?

Accepting someone as an acquaintance frees you both of emotional responsibility. This means you have interactions with this person or you just know of them but have very little if any, emotional ties. Stop making these people seem more than who they are.

Accepting someone as seasonal helps us respect their specific purpose in our lives. Their role is to come for a pre-destined period of time, so learn from your interaction with them and value the time they have already given.

Those we latch onto due to mutual acquaintance, we know and only interact with them because of a person we have in common. They serve us no purpose and we have no dealings with them outside of the mutual person. This is like the friend of a friend. We are not obligated to have an emotional connection to them

I've had to let go of some places. Recently I went to a club to celebrate a birthday with a friend. We had a lot of fun that day, just being together. But when I got home, I was reminded why I stopped going to that type of club. I was all sweaty, my hair and skin smelled of smoke and I felt disgusting. Once upon a time in my life, I was all for that type club. I've since outgrown that atmosphere and that crowd. I'm all for people enjoying themselves, having a good time. And I enjoy going to a laid back lounge sometimes, and occasionally a place to dance, but that particular type club is just not for me. Not anymore. Figure out what works for you and let go of the rest. Let go of what you outgrow.

I've had to let go of bad habits and make an effort to replace them with good ones. For example, I decided to stop storing alcohol in my home. I began to notice how I turned to it when I wanted to decompress or when I was stressed. I don't have a problem with an occasional drink, but it started to become a crutch. Anytime I was upset about something, I would turn to a drink rather than dealing with the issue at hand. In order to help myself, I decided I make it more difficult to access. One day I poured all of the alcohol down the drain, then started to find other ways to decompress like reading, writing, painting, yardwork, crafts or meditating. Sure, I can go to the store and by more, but in the emotional moment of weakness, I would have to leave my house, drive to the store, select a drink then drive back home, and just the thought of doing all that gives me time to reconsider.

We all have habits we need to purge. Whether it's smoking or eating badly or other negative behaviors, evaluate not only your habits but the reasons behind them. That allows you to identify triggers so you can purposely create new healthy habits.

The same goes for traditions and routines. Sometimes we keep traditions because they are comfortable for us and have been passed down to us by someone we care about. But do these traditions make sense and do they currently serve a purpose in your life? I'm told of a story of a woman who cut off the ends of her ham. When asked why, she said "because my mother always did it". She then asked her mother why this was done. The mother replied" Because I did not have a pan large enough for the whole ham to fit". It is perfectly fine to research traditions. You may find that some of them were merely habits that served a particular purpose but was adopted as permanent.

We adopt routines because it makes us feel secure, and even if we are not progressing, we sometomes continue those routines. Although routines are helpful at times, when they cause us to become stagnant and complacent, they need to be evaluated. Rather than following a routine, focus instead on accomplishing a specific goal.

Let go of negative thoughts like excuses and fear. Excuses are used in an attempt to explain why we haven't or won't do what we should be doing. I've been proud of myself many times for pushing through something that I did not want to or thought I could not do. Pushing through allows me to see the outcome and build my confidence, whereas, giving an excuse would have prevented me from achieving that goal. It also allows me to accept responsibility for my actions rather than pointing or dodging blame.

Let go of fear. Fear prevents us from accomplishing so much! It can also prevent us from even beginning. It steals your dreams and crushes your vision. It can prevent you from trying something new or doing something in a new way. Don't let fear be the reason you neglect to start, make you stop something you've started or slow you down. God did not give us the spirit of fear, so why let that stop you?

One thing I've learned that works very well for me. As soon as negative thoughts enter your mind, pause and imagine yourself physically fighting against those thoughts. As soon as they come, push them away. This has been very helpful in clearning my mind in preparation for testing, meditation, speaking, reliving negative memories or doing anything that requires confidence.

Sometimes it is hard to let go, so much to the point that we fight to hang on to people, places, and things that are no longer beneficial. Do an evaluation and decide what you need to keep, what needs to be removed or released, what's excess and then take action! Ask yourself, Is it fulfilling my needs or have I just settled? Is it a help or hinderance? Does it require more than what I have? Why am I holding on? What are my other options?

Purging allows you to truly appreciate right now. You are saying, *"You are important to me. This is important to me, and I embrace every moment, every blessing"*.

Most importantly, no one can purge for you. It's is a sacrificial effort.

CHAPTER THREE

Baggage

One day, I was observing people passing by. Most women had a purse, lunch bag, laptop bag, and misc bag. I started to wonder why do we carry so much? And how much of what we actually carry is necessary?

When traveling, we typically carry with us only the things we will need for that particular trip. Once we reach our destination, we use only what we need. Once we are done, we put everything away and store the bag until needed again. I have learned that overpacking becomes a burden and is heavy, and underpacking becomes stressful and I suffer lack.

How different is emotional baggage?

Are the things you carry helping or hurting you? Carrying some weight is helpful because it humbles us, builds muscle and gives us strength. But there is a limit. Too much weight can cause damage, and too little can cause stagnation. Although baggage is designed to hold whatever you put in it, you are the one who decides what goes, what stays.

Think of your mind and your heart as the bag. Most of us carry emotional baggage of some kind. Emotions are good to have, experience and feel. They guide us, affect our mood, our relationships and are just a part of who we are. A life without emotions is like traveling without luggage; you can go without but will be unprepared and temporary minded along the way. We need to learn how to deal with emotional baggage, what to keep, when to use, and how to unpack what we no longer need.

Allow yourself to feel the emotions as they come, but don't dwell in any one place. Emotions are tools to be used, not anchors to burden us. If we deny ourselves our true feelings, then we are denying ourselves reality. It's perfectly natural to get upset or sad about something. It's not normal, however, to remain in that state. Likewise, for happiness or "good feelings,". No one is always happy, and you shouldn't expect to. Life is a roller coaster of emotions, and we must allow ourselves to feel them all, then learn how to handle them.

Imagine someone hurt you and never apologized. They move on with their life, and you are still upset. Years later, the memory of them causes you to be presently upset, which changes your mood. This negatively affects your present situation. Emotional baggage is when you carry the hurt from the past and allow it to affect you today.

Imagine you worked really hard at your job, you applied for a position but was disappointed because you did not get it. Another position comes open that you are perfectly quaified for, but you don't apply out of fear of rejection. Years later, you are in the same position because you allowed the dissapointment to prevent you from attempting to advance any further. We give power to the person or situation that hurt us until we choose to release. When you let go, you regain your power and give yourself permission to experience life again.

Don't be afraid to love even if it hurts a little. Don't be afraid of pain; it is needed to grow. Don't be afraid of anger. It is what you do with your anger that matters. Just like a bag, if you try to hold on to too much, you will have to deal with the weight of carrying it all and you might bust. Although things may hurt, you must rise above what happened to you in order to be truly you.

Also, recognize what battles are yours to fight. Many of us are carrying ill feelings towards others because we got involved in a situation that has nothing to do with us. Carry only what belongs to you. We have enough of a battle dealing with our own concerns. Take with you only what you need. Frustration can be turned into hope. Disappointment can become experience and fear can be turned into anticipation. You alone are responsible for what you choose to carry.

CHAPTER FOUR

Self Esteem

"Not everyone can be famous but everyone can be great."
~Rev. Dr. Martin Luther King Jr,

WHO ARE YOU?

Do you realize whatever you say behind the words "*I Am*," you begin to believe?

For so long, my opinion of myself was based on someone else's reaction or approval of me. If they responded well, I was happy and if they responded negatively, I was upset. But that's a dangerous way to be. As opinions and preferences change, if you spend your life seeking to please others, you will be in a constant state of insufficiency and void.

Yes, others can help boost your confidence because they witness who you are and what you've done. After all, accolades are given as a result of something you earned, or accomplished, and although the acknowledgment and praises feel good, they should never be depended on to prove your worth. Do your best at all times because it is within your power to do so, regardless of others seeing or acknowledging you. Earn respect rather than seeking validation.

I've had to learn to examine myself, encourage and believe in myself. Being your authentic self, using your natural abilities, allow others to truly get to know you, and what you are capable of, only then can you trust their pure love for and admiration of you. Self-esteem is built by knowing and defining who you are, and by deciding to make a difference just by being you.

Your uniqueness has a purpose. Own everything about yourself. Your strengths, your weaknesses, your personality, your flaws, your trials, and accomplishments are all a part of you. Be proud of yourself. Be happy for yourself. Take chances. Learn. Build. Grow. Do. Be confident, but not arrogant. Resist the urge to compare yourself to other people's abilities and personalities and blaze your own path.

Yes, I've battled insecurities. But once I began to see myself the way God sees me, the insecurities no longer had a voice. Doubt has never been strong enough to stop me. Should a doubt arise within you, use it as motivation to figure out what you need to do. When you believe in yourself, it is easy for others to believe in you too!

I am beautiful, I am smart, I am capable, I am strong.

CHAPTER FIVE

Self-Control

Who influences you? Is it your family? Friends? Strangers?

What is stronger than you? Is it your mood? Your desires? Your fears?

Whose voice is louder than yours?

Whose dreams are brighter than yours?

If the answers to any of these questions are anything other than yourself, then you need to practice self-control. The phrase defines itself: *The ability to exercise restraint over your impulses, emotions, or desires.*

I am not a fan of judicial laws. It is my opinion that most people should be given the responsibility to determine for themselves what is best, then choose to do what is right. However, because we often look to others to guide us, and we don't always make the best decisions, sometimes there is a need to be given a set of "rules" or guidelines to follow. But we weren't created this way. Most of us have the ability to make the right choices and control ourselves.

I believe self-control is the strongest display of power you can have. It is the foundation and protection of your own self. It shows strength, character, principle, discipline, and it shows what you believe. If you have self-control, you cannot be moved, and you will not make a move without consideration.

If people, situations or circumstances change who you are, or the decisions you make, then you are allowing someone or something else to control you. You have to control your own thoughts, desires, and your mind, so you are able to make the best choices.

Self-control starts with knowledge and understanding, then displayed through making decisions to control yourself. Here are some things that can help you gain self-control:

- Know your weakness. This helps you set limitations. Limitations tell you not to eat too much, spend too much, speak too much or use the wrong words. Self-control in these situations helps you to calm your temper, go to bed at a decent hour, get to work on time or helps prevent putting yourself in temptational situations.

- Regain control of yourself. Address situations and thoughts that keep you under submission. If it is insecurity, seek knowledge. If it is an influence, change your circle. If it is fear, explore. If it's a substance or trauma, seek help. If it is conflict, get it resolved. Whatever holds you back, controls you, so take the steps to free yourself.

- Control your environment. When there are things in your life you identify as triggers or temptations for undesirable behaviors, you have to control those things as much as possible. Remove yourself from temptation. Stop bad habits. Surround yourself with positivity. Say no. Set limitations. Communicate boundaries.

Self-control is self-love. The refusal to control yourself is self-sabotage. Like when controlling a vehicle, once you've been given the keys, you must learn when to go, when to slow down, what direction you are headed, how to handle detours, how to dodge potholes and obstacles, and when to just stop. We have to know how to control our own life.

CHAPTER SIX

Conflict

I don't like to deal with confrontation. When faced with a situation, I either lash out I completely withdraw. Neither of these is proper. The best way is to deal with conflict is candidly but carefully and as it arises so we can rectify the situation and soon come to a mutual resolution.

As long as we live we will face conflict. Conflict does not have to be permanent nor result in a loss, it does not always mean to fight, and it does not always have to evoke anger. Unhealthy conflict is damaging. But it doesn't have to be that way. When handled correctly, conflict results in respect, confidence, and peace. Healthy conflict challenges who we are, what we believe, and how we think. Let's explore the difference between the two.

Sometimes conflict comes from within. Such as the battle of who you are versus who you're becoming. It can be the vision for your life versus what you settle for. It can be the battle of your strength, versus your fear. It can be the battle against your own temptations. It can be the battle of scars from your past. And itt can be the battle of comfort, versus growth.

You have not yet matured if your past still has influence over who you are now, or if you rebel against growth. When a situation arises, the old nature may want to react cowardly, harshly or recklessly, whereas, the new nature, being more settled, understands that the way a situation is handled can either feed the flame or put it out, it can push you towards your destiny or cause you to stumble. You know you have grown when the old (version of) you arises, but the current (version of) you take control of the situation.

Internal conflict can be relentless. I've been so hard on myself for making a mistake or a bad decision that I relive the moment repeatedly. This kind of conflict isn't good. Have you ever been disciplined physically or emotionally? If so, which did you dislike more?

Although we may prefer neither, in many cases, the physical pain eventually subsides, while the emotional pain can last long and can be relived repeatedly. When we do this to ourselves, there is little escape. We must learn how to fight against the things which weigh us down and not continually punish ourselves.

Unforgiveness is another type of conflict that can cause damaging behavior such as addiction, depression self-sabotage and violence. It may be easier only for a moment to run from the things that haunt us rather than dealing with the reality of them. However, in my experience, it is much more beneficial to feel the temporary pain of confrontation so you can find freedom. In order to let things go, confront the issue, learn from it and move on. You won't win the war against the world if you don't first win the war against your self.

When we have a conflict with others it is easy to want to isolate ourselves from the source and from the world, and hope it just goes away. But truth is, nothing goes away just by ignoring it, and nothing changes because we avoid it. If we don't address conflict as it occurs, it can cause more pain, resentment and an unnecessary ongoing battle.

When dealing with people, we can't be selfish, arrogant or temporary minded. Speak clearly and listen respectfully to the other person while understanding they too have a perspective, from a different point of view. Give them the same consideration you would want. The Golden Rule is a good thing. Treat people the way you want to be treated. Don't go to a person ready to attack instead, go to them ready to resolve.

We must be willing to confront and acknowledge our behavior and not give excuses or place blame. Likewise, we must be willing to unconditionally forgive. Once the issue is addressed you can rest with confidence you've done your part.

Not all conflict ends with reconciliation. You can't make a situation go away, and you can't control how it will end, but you can acknowledge and accept the results then move on. I've had some conflict end with mutual understanding, and I've had some cause more distance, but the distance is not necessarily a bad thing. If a conflict creates confusion, then separation is sometimes necessary.

The main idea is to find the root cause and address it so it does not resurface, even if it means you agree to disagree. When handled correctly it brings about strength and insight, which produces growth.

Relationships don't last because of the warm and fuzzy good times. They last because the difficult times were handled with care. You always know when a situation has been handled well because the end result is peace.

CHAPTER SEVEN

Freedom

Most things that control us are mentally and emotionally anchored. Everything from abuse, addiction, harmful habits, people's opinions, expectations, even guilt and regret can bind us. Anytime we consider the demands and expectations of others above our own; we are subjected to them. And anything preventing us from being our true self, oppresses us.

You were uniquely created with specific abilities. You have the power (ability) to break free and remain free from comparison and expectations of others. You have the power and the right to live how you want, think how you want, and be who you want. Freedom allows you to explore, create, and cultivate. It allows you the opportunity to make decisions for yourself.

Whether you are just beginning to define yourself or if you're in a difficult situation and have gone down the wrong path, you can be free. You can write your own story, you can stand up and turn around! Freedom is being yourself and refusing to allow yourself to be abused, mistreated or pressured into thinking, feeling, doing or acting a certain way. That's how people blackmail others, they threaten them in order to influence their behavior. Recognize the things that bind you so that you can break free.

Now, don't think just because someone disagrees with you or gives you limitations means you are being oppressed. We must respect rules and boundaries, but even with them, you are free to decide for yourself whether to comply. For example, if I come to your house, I am expected to show a certain level of respect of the house, the rules, and the people in it. I don't have to like the rules, and I don't have to even agree to them but I am also free to stay or leave. Likewise, as the head of household, you are free to decide how to best handle your home and anyone that who violates your space.

Although it is wise to consider other people and other contributors, final decisions are up to you. You are free to choose everything about yourself, your life and how you manage it all but freedom both a privilege and a duty and along with it comes responsibility. The purpose of freedom is so that we have the power to choose for ourselves.

So take your freedom and live! Think how you want, talk how you want, walk how you want, dress how you want, go where you want, live how you want, love how you want, dance how you want. Live every moment freely, with all power and courage, to do and be whatever and whomever you want. But remember, although we are free to choose, we are not free from the consequence, so choose wisely!

CHAPTER EIGHT

Motivation

Excerpts from my diary: *"I didn't always have the best youth. But regardless of the reality I was dealt, I came to the point when I had to decide what kind of life, I wanted for myself. I knew I wanted a life absent of the things unhealthy and unpleasant that plagued my past. I wanted a life that included things which cultivated my vision of peace. As we go through each day, we can choose to either be held back by the distractions or motivated by our vision. Each day, I make choices to push myself toward the vision. Each day, I CHOOSE LIFE."* ~Martina, April 18, 2016.

What gets you up in the morning? What keeps you going and pushes you toward your goal? What helps you to stay focused? Motivation. It is the drive, the reason we make certain choices, the thing keeping us on the right path. *So how do we stay motivated?*

Motivation is not always strong, and it's not always easy but we need it in order to reach our goals. We need it to get through life! Otherwise, our goals become dreams never achieved, and our life becomes filled with daily rituals, while we move aimlessly through it.

Figure out what works for you. Sometimes, it may be a song or a playlist, sometimes certain friends or people we can call on, or even a passage. Be thankful for the people and things who make us feel inspired, however, don't rely on them. Motivation is our own responsibility. Sometimes you have to find the strength within yourself.

We live in a world where we are constantly moving with constant demands and constant change. It's easy to get distracted and lose focus. We can come up with a number of excuses to explain why we aren't reaching our goal, but people, things, and circumstances should not cause us to lose sight of our vision.

Figure out what you want. What does it look like? What are the non-negotiables? What do you need? What do you want? Paint the picture.

I personally am a visual learner. I have to physically see reminders in front of me. I have to write things down and put them in a place I will constantly see. This does a couple of things for me. It reminds me of my vision, and it reminds me to focus on the daily tasks to push me toward my vision. Even if you don't have the full picture, you should have some idea of what you want or don't want.

I've created for myself a vision board. In one corner, I have written my goals. These are the things that I need in my life in order to fulfill my vision. In another corner, I have written my strengths. These remind me to celebrate the things that I already do well. In the third corner, I wrote my weaknesses. These keep me humble and remind me to focus on improvement. In the last corner, I wrote down the desires of my heart. Dream high and reach for the sky!

In the middle of the board, I wrote the title MOSAIC. It reminds me I must manage all of the pieces of my life and purposely create something beautiful. Yes, I can work very hard at achieving my goals, but I still have to put it all together to create a beautiful life.

Without vision, you wander aimlessly through life hoping things turn out well. Having a vision helps us remain focused and helps us to remember to take the steps daily that we need to reach our goals. Seeing my board right before I leave out the door reminds me to make wise choices, which will lead to wise habits and my goal of freedom. And it reminds me to focus and recognize opportunities as they come.

This also reminds me that in everything I say, consume, and do, I should choose the path that leads me towards the vision for my life. I let my vision guide me, mistakes teach me, and my pain motivate me. My focus must be greater than distractions.

Everything I am and everything I encounter is to be used. I have bricks, (things that were done to me, complications of life, circumstances, and difficulties) and windows (inspiration, motivation, and vision) to use. My goal is to build windows larger than my bricks. Therefore, every day I must work towards my goal.

Motivation alone won't help you reach your goals. It pushes you toward your goal but you still have to do the work. So you've got baggage? People have hurt and abandoned you. Does your life reflect your vision? Do your choices push you towards that vision? If not, then use those things as your motivation. Take up your bed and walk, and find ways to enjoy the journey!

CHAPTER NINE

Image

Artists and designers specialize in creating images. Photographers specialize in capturing images. Images are visual representations of something. Every day we are artists who create images of ourselves that stimulate the visual perception others capture of us.

There are things that tell others about you before you ever speak. How are you dressed? Do you walk upright with confidence? What tone do you speak? Do you use encouraging words? Are you upbeat and positive? Or are you unkempt? Do you walk with your head and shoulders down? Are you messy and loud? Do you participate in conflict and are a complainer?

These are two perspectives of your image I want to address, both the image we would like present of ourselves, and the image others actually see. Have you ever taken a selfie then thought oh my goodness, let me retake that? That's because you would like the image you create to match the image that's actually captured.

The image you purposely create for yourself, you can control. Think of your image as your personal logo, or your advertisement. When artists design a logo it is done with the intent of creating an image for others to identify. The logo tells a brief story, it is the face of what you are trying to sell. Once you decide what image you want to carry, the things you wear, how you act and what you do, contribute to that image.

Before you wear something, ask yourself, "What message do I want to send and does this outfit support that?" Another contributor is the way we choose to groom. Although the way you wear your hair shows your personality, you need to know what side of your personality to show and when to do so. For example, you wouldn't want to wear a moussed six-inch spiked Mohawk, nor a neon-streaked bob to a managerial job interview.

There are other things like the type and amount of jewelry we wear, the amount of makeup we put on and even the length or fit of our clothes that shows our personality. No one can see your intentions, your dreams nor your struggles; they can only see your appearance, the way you carry yourself and your actions.

Then there is the perception others have of you. Besides the way you dress, the way you walk, talk, the places you go, the way you handle your affairs, the way you handle conflict, your attitude and your mannerisms contribute to the image others have of you.

Both your appearance and your actions are seen by others. First impressions matter, but images are usually built off of repeat encounters and observances. Keep in mind that even if you do not personally interact with someone, they may have an image of you. So many times, upon my first official meeting with someone I am often told, *"Oh, I already know who you are."* This makes me even more aware of myself.

When creating your personal image, think about who you are, and who you aspire to be. How do you want people to view you? Don't compare yourself to anyone and don't try to mimic another person. Take your personality and create an image which represents you. Don't obsess over creating an image so much that you lose the essence of who you really are. Instead, display to the world who you are.

I've come to realize I am me and in all this world there is none other like me. I am unique, and I express myself as such.

CHAPTER TEN

Style

Excerpts from my diary:

'Sunshine" is what they call me. No matter the weather, or the time of day, they come looking for Sunshine. A coworker started calling me that, then the name just remained. One day I asked, *"Why do you call me Sunshine? Is it because I open the windows and bask in the sun?* "No," he said. *"It is because, no matter what mood I am in, I am guaranteed to have a brighter day just by passing your way."*

Your style is how you do what you do. It's your twang, your thang, your way, your signature. The way you walk, the way you talk, and the way you dress are all reflective of you. Your style, follows you, becomes you, and introduces you.

You are guaranteed to go through several phases before figuring out your style. It's like going into a fitting room and trying on multiple items then deciding what is right for you. Of all the choices, some may look good, feel good, some you have been told are good, is trendy, but may not be good for you.

Once you find something that fits, go with it. But you're not stuck to it. Your style will evolve as you mature. What you wore as a teenager and the way you carried yourself is not the same as when you're in your twenties or thirties and beyond. Decide what makes you look and feel good, what allows you to express yourself and what works for you. This also applies to life. The way we handle each day and the way we handle things that come our way are our styles. Once your style is defined, come rain or shine, you will still be you.

I don't always have good days. As a matter of fact, on some days it takes a tremendous effort just to get out of the bed. I am a person who feels every emotion, which sometimes is a blessing and other times overwhelming. Nevertheless, I get up and face every day, every challenge, that sometimes takes me on a roller coaster of a ride. I used to try and force myself to be more "stable" and choose which emotion I wanted to deal with until I learned to just embrace who I am and face my challenges as they come.

I've learned to take everything that comes my way and deal with it, then press on. I can't deny myself any of the emotions because they are a part of who I am. Instead, I need to control them, which means I have to learn what to do with what I feel, as I feel it. The longer you let something hide, the bigger a problem it becomes, and when I hide my true feelings, they manifest in unhealthy ways at unexpected times.

Not everyone has the same style. That's the whole intent of this book. To get you to look at your life and figure out what you need to do in order to fully embrace who you are and pull all the pieces together. Define yourself then outwardly and unapologetically express yourself. I am a unique embracer of self, a loving light, effortlessly captivating. My laughter brings joy, conversation as deep as the sea and hopes as high as the sky. I'm a natural beauty, rooted and grounded in wisdom that I know how to use. I'm like silk thread, smooth, yet strong enough to hold things together, yet gentle enough to break away. I'm a woman full of passion and inspiration. I have a hand with a grip to hold close, yet a touch as gentle as a cool breeze on a summer day.

Your style is the way you approach things, the way you flow, the way you work, the way you carry yourself. My style is love. I love passionate. I love hard. I love purely.

CHAPTER ELEVEN

Character

Your character is "who" you are, defined by your choices and your actions.

At some point, regardless of training and upbringing, you have to choose who you will be and how you will handle your life. Yes, our family and history set the foundation for our lives, however, we are unique individuals with a specific design and in order for us to truly glorify God, we must live up to the fullest potential of who He wants us to be.

There will come a time that you will have to release some teachings and traditions, learn some new things, break some chains and hold yourself accountable. You must focus on building and sustaining your character. Question to ask yourself is: "*Who am I?*"

One aspect of your character is consistency. Your life should reflect who you are and what you believe. Someone should be able to know when something is not right with you; when they notice something out of your normal character. I've had people say "*That's not like you, are you okay today?*".

Developing your character also requires healthy communication. Create an image for yourself, have a personal style and take pride in who you are and what you do. Set boundaries and be intentional about your choices.

The way you run your life contributes to your character and either uplift or detracts from it. You have control over who you choose to be. I've had to decide what I like, what I don't like, what I believe, and what I will and will not do. Some things went against my upbringing and some embraced it. I had to decide how to handle my life as a whole. I like to say "Can't nobody do me like me". Your Character is built, respect and trust are earned, and all are displayed through consistency and example.

Your character is defined by you and matured by you. I'm not perfect. I never will be perfect. I don't want to be perfect. Perfection is an unrealistic, unnecessarily stressful illusion. It is based on external desires and anchored in expectation. It is shallow, damaging, and dependent on interpretation. Perfection aims to mimic someone else's interpretation and loses the essence of you. It is binding. It is blinding. Perfection cannot be explained because it cannot be attained. When developing your character, allow yourself to appreciate God's grace. God does not expect us to he perfect. He just desires that we live to the highest standard a life that is upright and true. Rather than trying to be perfect, just be real, be true, be you! Define who you are and walk unapologetically.

CHAPTER TWELVE

Health

When I was younger, I never thought much about my health. I could do what I wanted when I wanted, if I wanted. I ate what I wanted, stayed up as late as I wanted, and never had the slightest concern. I had great health and tons of energy! As I got older, I realized that I need to take better care of myself. I don't want to have an illness concern come my way in order to be more aware of my choices, and it's wise of me to put in the work to maintain good health now.

When you are healthy, you feel better, and it makes life much easier to enjoy. Your body is the vessel which carries you, and you are responsible for taking care of it. It is important to make the right choices to put you on the path to a healthy lifestyle. Regardless of your health condition, gaining control now puts you in a better position later.

I've had no major problems or illnesses. I visited the doctor only for yearly well care visits so, for the most part, I felt I could do whatever I wanted and still get good results. But then there came a time I understand differently. My awakening came after an unexpected double surgery. I broke my leg and had abdominal surgery a week apart! I couldn't put weight on my broken leg nor my abdomen, so I had to rely on a walker for almost six weeks.

During that time, many of my habits changed. A couple of those habits were food and rest. My portion sizes shrank, I ate fruit rather than junk food, I drank mostly water, and I rested more, both by sleeping and sitting down. I ended up losing twenty pounds!

As I started to recover though, I noticed myself returning to some of my habits, and also returned some of the weight. That's when I began to realize how much control I had over my health, and what habits were working against me. It's not necessarily that I was making bad choices, but I wasn't making the best ones. I noticed how some of the junk food I ate caused me to be sluggish and the caffeine I drank enhanced my mood swings. These things I did not recognize when I was consuming them constantly, but once they were re-introduced into my system, it was easier for me to see the effect.

Learn your habits and limitations, but most of all, recognize the need to get healthy and stay healthy. Know your body, address any condition you have and take steps to maintain good health. There are national standards for a healthy body, but you should always know what your "normal" is particularly for you so you have a baseline to compare should anything change.

Pay attention to the way your body reacts when you consume or or participate in certin things. Everything is not for everyone. If you are able to participate in or consume something, know your limitation and when you've had enough.

If you deal with illness of any kind, although we cannot always control the onset of illnesses, and we cannot always change the condition itself, we should always make the best choices to lead us towards good health, and whenever possible, prevention.

It's always a great idea to detox, and rid your body of toxins and unhealthy chemicals. Some things are like addictions. Smoking and drinking are just a couple addictions we battle. In my case, it was easy for me to walk away from almost everything except caffeine. It gave me headaches the day I went without. I had to purposely schedule time to allow my body to push through the headaches and rest. Once the headaches were over, I had to resist replacing the caffeine with other damaging things and I had to break the habit of needing a drink.

Your body not only responds to the things put in it but also the things put on it. Everything from lotions, perfumes, and makeup, in addition to food and things we ingest all are absorbed by your body and affect your health. Balance what you eat, drink and do. Pay attention to ingredients and buy natural products when possible. Yes, it is easy to skip or substitute healthy options for something we prefer but remember, you only get one body so you can either take care of it now or you will have to deal with the results later. Allow yourself a cheat meal or a snack, but know your limitations and don't become dependant on unhealthy choices or suffer a relapse.

I notice when I would eat a snack on the weekend, it made me crave soemthing from the vending machine at work, then before I knew it, Iwas replinishing snacks at home and the cycle continued. I started buying crispy fruit and vegetables. This satisfied the need for crunch that I seek, while occupying my need to chew and doing so in a healthier way.

Being healthy is a lifestyle. Every choice you make contributes to that lifestyle. Once you commit to being healthy, knowledge, discipline and self-control are a huge benefit. Temptations, social conditioning, and unhealthy habits must then go. There are so many facets to good health and so much advice on getting and staying healthy. Learn what works for you and take the steps towards a goal of a healthy life!

CHAPTER THIRTEEN

Soul

I like to describe the soul as the person you are when the entire world quiets down, the lights are low, no one is around and you listen to yourself. It's your essence. It's your true voice. It works alongside your mind and your body, and the condition of it can either work together or in opposition. A healthy soul makes it much easier to control your mind and steer your body. The question is, *How do I fulfill my destiny and how do I figure out my path?*

To begin, take out the time on a regular basis to quiet down and hear yourself. We can get so caught up in constant stimulation that it can drown out our inner voice and crush us into tiny hopeless pieces.

You are important. Whatever you think, feel, desire are unique to you and you must be absolutely unapologetic about who you are. When we deny ourselves the opportunity to just be ourselves, we are destroying the core of our existence. In every stage of your life, of the things you learn and the things you master, you are who you are. Own your life, your journey and every piece of your puzzle.

Do you remember the days of childhood when we had hopes and dreams? Dreams of becoming, dreams of a life we wanted? What happened to those dreams? Do you wake up every day thinking of a life you'd rather have or a way you'd rather be?

Even if we aren't living the life we dream of right now, there's always an opportunity to reach for that. Every mistake is for growth, and every triumph is to be celebrated. You must believe that you deserve to live your life the way you were created to, and you can do, and be whatever and whomever you want.

Learn how to love freely. Learn how to give and earn trust. Learn how to be at peace, practice patience and embrace growth. Search within yourself, let go of the things that bind you and cultivate your strengths. Get to know who you really are.

God created you unique and for a specific purpose. Although the world around us has lots to contribute to who we are, God has already written a destiny for you. The footprints are in your soul guiding you eacy step of the way. Give honor to wisdom and guidance, but also to the voice of God that will sometimes pull you aside to speak to you individually and guide you on a special path.

We should strive to become so familliar with the voice of God that every contrary voice is inaudible.

CHAPTER FOURTEEN

Unapologetic

I've been through a lot, seen a lot, and I've done a lot. Some of my story have been told. Some things I've done have witnesses. Some things I have forgotten and they remain hidden, and some things are as fresh in my memory as if they happened yesterday. I don't deny my past, and I don't walk blindly in my present. I don't mask who I am. I recognize who I am. I've grown and I've changed.

I've spent too much time in the shadows of those who prefer I be different. Now when I look in the mirror, I see myself for who I am. I love my mind, my body, and my spirit. I can finally stare into the depths of my soul and embrace myself, flaws and all. Yes, it would be easy to hide and cover up, but what do I accomplish by being who I'm not? Scars are beautiful. Flaws are real. To some, they hold painful memories, but for me, they are reminders of where I've come. I have learned that you cannot outrun yourself, because wherever you turn you will still be there.

I'm not perfect and I don't aim to be. I've made mistakes, bad decisions, deliberate choices, and choices that no one understood but me. I've been focused and I've been distracted. In all of the layers of me, you decide what you want to see. But when you see me, however, KNOW that I am who I am. I don't have to introduce it. I can't deny it, and I won't change. The fact that I have been through the storm and have evolved into this version of myself is amazing to me. Yes, I am continuing to grow, but I truly admire who I am today.

There were times in my life when I would focus on my blemishes and the scars of my past. I would deny myself the opportunity to truly live. But then I realized that not only have I survived, but I am also blooming. The path my life has taken me on has been a turbulent one indeed, but it has prepared me for such a time as this. I now have the strength and grace to handle the life I have left.

It's a great disservice to look back and see how far I've come just to be discouraged and quit now. I am a like a jigsaw puzzle. There are many pieces of me, but only those with patience enough to assemble all of the pieces can appreciate the final portrait. When I piece together a puzzle, I start with the outer edges working inward towards the intricate details and I will not pretend I am anything less to figure out, but I know I am worth it.

I've learned how to handle myself, and my business. I've apologized when I needed to, confronted what I needed to, closed doors and walked through open ones. I've explored, I've learned, I've grown. I left where I didn't belong, traveled, changed, purged, and kept what I needed. I stepped up, stepped back, stepped out and stepped in. I've both complied and rebelled. I've created and destroyed, and I have broken and repaired.

I'll never be good enough for some, and others will always find something wrong, but I don't wear any of those opinions on my sleeve. I spent too many years trying to prove who I am, so I won't waste any more time.

I smile at my past, cry at my past and laugh at my past, but most of all, I've learned from my past. I've been mad, happy, sad and proud. Everything I am, and what I will be, is comprised of what I once was. I am intricately and unapologetically me! ♡

CHAPTER FIFTEEN

Power

Power is bigger than education, bigger than popularity, bigger than words, bigger than ego. It stands strong and confident, and it has something to bring to the table. When a powerful person walks into a room, they don't announce their power. Instead, they demonstrate it. Power requires strength and knowledge. Sure, you can be strong, but do you know how to use your strength? You are knowledgeable, but do you have the strength to make it through? We all have a certain amount of power. Use who you are and what you have to elevate yourself to the next level.

Power is similar to playing a video game. Do you ever notice how the character must master a series of obstacles before they can complete the level? And at each level, the obstacles are more frequent and more difficult? If you fail, you begin again until you are strong enough and have enough knowledge to pass to the next level.

During the game, the character uses a combination of skill, speed, and strength to progress. He earns more tools to help him along the way, and he learns how to overcome challenges while being faced with new ones. He continues his journey motivated by the end result. He has perseverance. Only when he has mastered his skill and strength does he have the power to make it to the end and claim what he has earned.

So is life. So is our power. It's required for you to get stronger and wiser each level. All mental, physical and spiritual power is to be understood, strengthened, and used. Strength is built, using the tools given to us along the way. Trials make us stronger and choices make us wiser. When we learn to use our strength and wisdom, we show our power.

Sometimes the power is used to defeat an enemy, break down barriers, or capture something. And sometimes it's used to help us overcome and endure. Never underestimate your power. Run the race, conquer the obstacles, defeat the enemies, use your power, and claim your prize.

CHAPTER SIXTEEN

Cultivate

One of my favorite quotes is one often repeated by my father. *"Don't worry about the mule being blind, just load the wagon and shake the line."*

I did not understand that in my youth, but as I got older, I realized he was talking about responsibility and faith. We are responsible for doing our part then we must have faith that what needs to happen will. Trust the process. This chapter is dedicated to one of my favorite blogs I wrote while loading my wagon (tilling my land to plant a garden).

I was tending my yard one day, pulling weeds and planting seeds. As I kept digging, I realized how this compares to life. Sometimes we notice a seemingly harmless weed (weakness) that irritates us at most. We "nip it in the bud" and feel good for a while until it surfaces again. It's not until you attempt to cultivate something good, that you realize how deep a seemingly harmless weed is rooted.

This applies to mental, physical, spiritual, emotional work. Sometimes you have to dig deep to find every root (reason) and dig it all the way up so they won't affect the healthy things you grow. Sometimes you may get dirty, tired and frustrated, but do your best to identify and remove everything that does not belong so you can make room for the new and healthy.

Digging is sometimes hard work., but don't get discouraged. Once you put in the work and see the fruit of your labor, God gets the glory. And he will send us encouragement along the way.

One day my daughter was outside with me using her own tools, and her own perspective. While I was digging out the bad roots, stones, weeds, and branches, she was showing me "treasures" she found, including small flowers and pretty leaves. That reminded me, while we are cultivating and weeding out the bad, God's beauty can still shine.

Her question of the day was this, "Mommy, is the whole point of life for us to have fun"? I said, "Well kinda honey, we should enjoy life in ways that glorify God". She said, "So if you are having fun, does it mean you are glorifying God"? I said, "Not all fun glorifies God, but when you do things that glorifies God, it's kind of like having fun".

I still haven't been successful in growing a garden, but I have now successfully grown a few plants. I don't know how much more work I will have to put in or what other hidden roots or hidden treasures I will find when I try again, but I know it all starts with cultivating (cleaning and preparing) the land.

I learned a few things here:

Lesson One: The first thing we should do is become obedient to the obvious things, the things we know we should already be doing. Pluck (purge) out the bad. We cannot expect God to reveal more to us when we haven't followed what He has already shown us. Before God gives you direction in the "important" things, you must first be obedient with the "small" things.

Lesson Two: Pray and continually seek God's wisdom and guidance in everything you do. People have opinions, but it is God who made you and he made you unique so he should be the master teacher and will show you what you need to do to prepare for what he has for you.

Lesson Three: Rearrange your priorities so your primary motivation is to glorify God. Begin with the end in mind. That way, you won't cut corners, and you will give it your best effort. Whether my garden grows or not, I sure feel better knowing the weeds have been plucked and stones removed!

Lesson Four: Saturate yourself with the Spirit of God. Take out the time to listen to him and feel Him guide you. Sometimes meditation can help you drown out the voices so that you can hear God clearly.

Lesson Five: We all should have someone who can give us advice and be real with us and give us a different perspective. Not only someone willing to work alongside us, but to encourage us along the way.

Lesson Six: Put in the work! Nothing comes from wishing. You have to do your part!

Once you do your part, practice patience. We may not always see the results of our hard work and if we do, it may not be right away, however, trust that if you do your part, the rest will be taken care of.

Cultivate your life! Purge the bad, make room for the good, then watch God's work!

CHAPTER SEVENTEEN

Love

"Love is a decision, not a feeling." ~Tarina W.

We all want to be loved unconditionally, but the problem is, we don't quite understand what it means. We don't understand how to give love, and we don't know how to receive love. With so many interpretations and misunderstandings of love, it's often abused.

Many times, we seek the image of love that gives us warm and fuzzy feelings, but it's so much more. Love is difficult to capture into words because words are limiting and true love is unimaginable and incomparable. In fact, this chapter is the shortest, though it took me the longest to write. Love hurts, is intricate, requires work, and is confusing. Yet, the pull towards love is real, and the benefits outweigh the difficulties.

Love can hurt, love can cause pain, love can be frustrating, and love can be consuming. When we are heartbroken or disappointed, it can bring us sadness and cause us to have a negative perception. But on the other side, love can be beautiful!

Do you ever notice how when you're in love your life changes? Your face is brighter, your eyes are wider, your smile is bigger, and you walk different too! Your walk becomes peppier, your back straightens, head held higher, and have a little more swag. Your voice gets kinder, your tone more sensitive, and your patience stronger. This is the reason why people are sometimes attracted to those who are already in relationships. You radiate happiness!

Love is, smiling at the thought of someone. Love is lyrics to a song and only that someone has the rhythm to flow with your beat. Love is feeling the presence of someone who's nowhere near you. Love is never counting time, seeing past flaws, and never holding mistakes. Love is an unexplainably perfect touch. Love is comfort without words. Love is accepting someone for who they are. Love is growing with someone. Love is perseverance. Love is enduring. Love is sacrificial. Love is a priority. Love is confident. Love is secure. Love is protective. Love is not wanting to change you, but wanting to change with you. Love takes effort. Love is never wanting to stop learning new things about you. Love is attentive. Love is calming. Love is the way you look at me. Love is considerate. Love cherishes. Love is honoring every stage of your life. Love is understanding. Love is transparent. Love breaks chains. Love is, even when I am upset with you I still want you by my side. Love is wanting to be better. Love is the ability to pull someone from a dark place. Love changes. Love stabilizes. Love has boundaries, but not limitations. Love is wanting the best for you, even if it's not me.

Love does not always mean happiness, but real love makes you smile, and makes you happy as a result! In all the loving you do, make sure the person at the top of the list is you!

CHAPTER EIGHTEEN

Trust

Excerpts from my diary:

"Do you trust me?"

"Every way there is."

I want to trust God the way my children trust me. My children will boldly ask me to do or give them something, knowing they are not perfect, but also knowing grace is sufficient. Whether small or large, they ask without hesitation. After making their request known, they leave, having full confidence that the request will be fulfilled. Then they patiently wait on its manifestation.

Believing in, depending on and having confidence in someone is a blessing. There is sweet relief in having someone you can trust completely. It's hard to get through this life without trust, yet it seems so elusive. But no matter how skeptical we may be, trust is easier than you think.

Trusting others on a basic level is easy. If you go to seek professional help, it's because you believe in their ability or knowledge to produce specific results. For example, if you go to the doctor and tell him your symptoms, you trust he will correctly diagnose you and can help you with treatment. If he prescribes medicine or remedy, you trust he is prescribing the correct one and clearly communicating the information on the script. You go to the pharmacy and trust them to give you the right prescription, and instructions on how you should take it.

We do this in many professions. You trust the teachers will educate your children, the banker to care for your money, and that the utility company has correctly reported your usage. You trust the drivers will stay in their lane, and you trust the random person who gives you directions.

You also put your trust in things. You trust the gas pump is properly counting gallons and the substance is really gas. You trust your car will get you to your destination, your bed will hold strong and your employer will pay what you've earned. You trust the computer will honor your commands, the ATM will give you correct cash and the remote will change the channel. We've grown so accustomed to the function of certain roles and things, that we automatically trust they will work as planned.

What these people and things have in common is the belief they will produce what you are expecting. But even if any of these fail, most of the time, rather than refusing to go to another doctor or pharmacy or drive another car or save and invest your own money, you address each instance at that moment, then trust it won't happen again.

So why is it so hard for us to trust people? Many times when we are disappointed, betrayed, used and abused, or if things don't work out as expected, we are broken. When we have failed relationships and broken promises, we wonder, *"How do I trust again?"*. It's easy to trust someone to do their job or an item to serve its purpose, but it's much more difficult to trust someone with your life and the matters of your heart.

The heart is such a strong yet delicate thing. Is that why it's called the heartbeat? As a matter of fact, when I think about a heart, I think warm and happy, and when I think of beat, I think of pain. Put them together, and it is indicative of the bittersweet challenges of the heart; the rhythm of our life.

Disappointment can cause us to mistrust and have a cynical outlook on life. If I don't trust you, I will never look at you the same, talk to you the same, interact with you the same, I will not build with you or plan with you. If I don't trust you, I treat you with skepticism. If I don't trust you, I don't believe you will stay and I won't give you a permanent place in my heart.

Rather than using disapointment as a learning experience, we tend to shut down and deny ourselves the freedom to trust anyone ever again. This is a form of self-punishment. The encounter is long gone and you are left isolated, broken and bitter. Even if you decide to trust, it is sometimes with reluctance, skepticism or with partiality.

I would love to tell you the magic remedy to trust again, but the truth is, I'd much rather be numb, protected and secured than to ever feel the pain of heartbreak again. I would much rather go through life alone than to trust someone else with my heart, mind, body or my soul, in fear of reliving one more painful moment. It hurts less, it feels safer, and it protects. However, when we do this, not only do we protect ourselves from hurt, harm, and danger, but we also isolate ourselves from those who want to love us purely.

Trust should be earned and protected. It doesn't mean you give people free rein to do whatever they want, or permission to treat you any kind of way. It does not mean that you interact with them blindly. It doesn't mean you jump all the way in without question, and it doesn't even mean you forget the pain. It means you open the door, and allow what will happen naturally, to happen. Once someone shows you they are not trustworthy, believe them, but don't let them overshadow those who are honest. Many honest people pay the price for someone else misleading.

The wonderful thing about trust is that it gives you a certain level of freedom. It's a beautiful thing to have someone you can talk to about anything, who is honest with you, has your back when you're right and challenges you when you're wrong. Someone who is there because they want to be and you know you're safe with them. I always say the ideal man of mine is one who can be in a room full of naked women and I know without a doubt he is tempted by none and only has eyes for me.

Trust is being comfortable enough to be completely myself without worry or stress and knowing that you accept me as is. There is beauty in knowing that someone values you that way.

When you decide to trust, you will be disappointed again, hurt again and you may not get what you expect. But you will also be surprised, experience love, and meet some good people. The point is, you cannot live in protective mode never trusting anyone because if you do, you will miss out on so many good things. When you trust people, it's not that you are guaranteed, nor are you always going to have a happy ending, but you have given yourself the freedom to try and trust them and trust yourself.

Trust the process. It may hurt, and it may be difficult, and it may take time, but believe that one day somehow, all of this will make sense. Although can't control the outcome, we can have faith things will work out!

Trust yourself! Part of a bird's ability to fly is the strength to do so, and the other part is believing it can be done.

Trust God. He has gotten you thus far. Through the transitions and various stages, through insecurities, through growth, he has imparted knowledge. He has strengthened our abilities and has matured our ways. Look back on where you've come, practice patience with where he is taking you and do not worry about the future, for tomorrow, today will be yesterday.

CHAPTER NINETEEN

Peace

Peace is not the absence of difficulties, but rather freedom and tranquility in the midst of it all. This peaceful place, we should be able to go to no matter where we are. It's a mental space that relieves us of life's pressures. Whether it's a song or reading, meditation or prayer, find out what works for you. This chapter is dedicated to my cleansing prayer for peace. When I wrote this, it is after I paused to acknowledge that only when we are focused on the end result, rather than the obstacles, we will achieve peace.

> Dear God,
>
> I submit myself to you and ask you to help me glorify you. Give me strength, wisdom, patience, righteousness, and integrity. Help me to be kind, longsuffering and honest. I pray for healthy communication that I will listen wholeheartedly and speak thoughtfully.
>
> I desire to be a better teacher, student, and nurturer. I desire your presence, guidance, wisdom, and correction in every aspect of my life, notwithstanding anything.
>
> You know my thoughts, fears, dreams, and tears. Help me to see the promise in each challenge I face. I trust you to lead and guide me. I cannot do this alone. Help me to recognize, not just in words, but also in choices that YOUR will be done.
>
> Each breath I take gives me the strength knowing that you are by my side. Not as a crutch but as one who created me and that knows what's best for me. I don't strive to be perfect, but to be an example of your grace

working within me. When I am distracted, help me focus. As I face each new challenge, give me strength.

I want to be free from negative thoughts, mistakes of my past, my hurts, and my disappointments, free from fear, my tears, guilt, and shame. I release everything holding me, both the known and unknown, never to be given power over me again. I reclaim my body and my mind!

I am ready to be transformed, mind, body, and soul. Your will is perfect, and I accept it for my life. I want to look at myself through your eyes and see every flaw, every truth, and all the potential, which means I must continually grow. I accept that I have to change what's comfortable, what's familiar and challenge what I think I know.

Today I step in faith that you will fertilize good seed within me, and I am forever grateful for even the thorns that remind me it is much deeper than what "I want" to do.

It is your power within me that gives me peace.

CHAPTER TWENTY

Patience

One thing I have learned and am continuing to remind myself is to slow down, stop rushing, and just be patient! Life would be so much easier if we take time out to understand this!

If I slow down driving, I'm more relaxed when I arrive.

If I slow down walking, I can enjoy the view

If I slow down talking, I can better communicate.

If I listen, I'm less likely to misunderstand.

If I slow down thinking, I can enjoy the moment.

If I slow down eating, I can actually taste my food.

If I slow down relationships, I can actually build them.

Stop trying to force things to work. Either it does, or it does not. The right things will happen in God's time. Stop trying to speed up the process. Some things need to mature. Stop wishing time away. Enjoy the time you have already been given.

Waiting to make certain purchases would have saved me debt. Waiting to make decisions would have spared me regret. Waiting to say yes would have saved me heartache. Waiting to jump would have saved me a headache.

If you have impulsive tendencies, take cash only with you to the store so you are forced to a budget. If you tend to shop online, place your card in a place difficult to get to. Then ask yourself:

Do I need this? And if so, do I need it right now?

In conversation, before you respond, take time to think. Say the words first to yourself, then ask yourself must I say that right now?

If I am patient, I can understand it is not time yet.

If I am patient, I can see progress.

If I am patient, I can enjoy life

Just as a child cannot feel himself grow to be a man, it happens regardless. This should help us understand everything happens in due time and just like a child cannot wish his age to be greater, so can we not wish our situations be expedited. Take the time, slow down, wait your turn.

Patience is not something you achieve instantly. It is a lifelong practice!

When I am patient, I have peace.

CHAPTER TWENTY-ONE

Growth

Sometimes I look at old photos of myself and remember what was going on at that time in my life. Then I smile and think wow, I've come a long way! I've come so far that people who know me now hardly believe the stories of how I once was and people that knew me back then look at me in awe of how far I've come! Growth is an amazing thing that you can't always see as it's happening, but as you look back, you can surely recognize progress!

As long as we live, we will grow. Every person we meet and every encounter we face are opportunities to learn and practice something new. These interactions can even teach us more about ourselves.

What was the last thing you did to help or allow yourself to grow? We have not seen all, gone all places, heard all, spoken to all people, tried it all, experienced it all and we do not know it all. There's an undiscovered world around us with opportunities we can't even imagine. Our experiences are limited to what we have been exposed to, but there is so much more to see. Even in our immediate space, there are new perspectives to hear and new information to learn.

- Social growth is learning about environment and cultures other than what we are comfortable with.

- Spiritual growth involves seeking answers and asking questions to mysteries.

- Personal growth, you discover what you like and don't like, your abilities and your thoughts. With personal growth, it is not the ability to remember, repeat and perform, but rather, it's the ability to discover and decide what you believe and what's best for you. It's the ability to conquer your greatest fears and your largest demons.

Growth causes change. It is recognizing who you once were

versus who you've become. Even if something works, there's always room to improve. Sometimes good enough is just not good enough! Continuous progress is key.

Life is a series of stages, like a tadpole to frog, caterpillar to butterfly and infant to elder. Every day is a step towards the evolution of you. You have to get outside your comfort zone in order to know how much larger life can be. Change involves becoming something completely different or improving what already works. Take responsibility for your own life. Figure out what works for you.

Growth isn't easy. You will have difficult moments, and when you do, if the tears should fall, let them fall. But when you cry, don't cry to quit, cry to keep going; then refocus and press on. Put forth the effort and keep going no matter where life takes you. Growth equals progressive change with visible results. Keep trying!

Once you grow, you will change, and the person you once were will no longer exist.

CHAPTER TWENTY-TWO

Communication

Communication shows respect. I was well into my adulthood before I realized I had communication issues. I thought of myself as a pretty good communicator. I could talk to almost anyone about almost anything. I could usually find the words to get my point across, had pretty good dialogue and diverse conversational skills. I also considered myself a good listener. Many people came to me to tell me stories, ask advice, or just have a listening ear. It was an honor to be chosen to listen and for them to eagerly await my response. It was like people turned to me with anticipation of, *"What is she going to say"*?

It's an honor to be chosen to hold many stories, many secrets, to give advice and to see people's faces light up as if to say, "*Someone gets it! Someone understands! Someone can relate!*". I had gotten so used to talking and listening, it became second nature to me. It was to the point that in conversation I expected myself to have something "wise" to say, and if I didn't, it felt like I was doing them a disservice. I then realized there should be a balance. It's perfectly fine for me to not have anything to say. It is perfectly fine for me to not respond and not even have an opinion.

Sometimes communication is not saying anything at all. Sometimes communication is listening to the other person enough for them to feel valued and for you to learn a thing or two. Sometimes communication is pausing to take a breath and see what, if anything, is the best thing to say. A pause will give you the right words or the right spirit to say it in. A pause may also tell you to wait before you say anything at all. Sometimes communication equals consideration. It will cause you to think, "Before I say something, is it necessary? And if so, how do I say it"? Just because I think it, does not mean I have to say it. Just because they said something to me does not mean I have to respond. Discretion lets us know what to say, when to say it and is usually activated with a simple pause.

I'm not saying to never speak up or to always second guess yourself. I'm not saying an immediate response isn't acceptable. What I am saying is communication is a two-way street, or rather even, three-dimensional as explained below. Wisdom helps us know the difference.

Part One- Talking.

Say exactly what you mean. Own your feelings and thoughts. Be authentically you. This is how people will get to know you. Be truthful. Changing what you mean or holding back in order to spare feelings, or be "politically correct," is insincere.

Sometimes, when I speak and listen to my own words, it's therapeutic! While writing this book, every word came flying back at me. I now understand myself on a completely different level. Once I began to connect what I thought to my words and my actions, I began to see myself differently. Writing also causes me to evaluate what I really mean versus what I'm saying. It causes me to evaluate what I am saying in comparison to my actions. This book has really changed the way I think, feel and act.

So many times I've written my thoughts then read and re-wrote. Then days would go by and I would re-read then re-write again because the words did not flow the way I intended. Oh, how grand life would be if we got a second chance on verbal conversations! If only we could press the delete key or the undo button and take back or say something differently! And sometimes reading my own words have helped me to understand why someone may have gotten upset at or misunderstood something I was trying to say.

Have you ever gone back through your text messages or emails and re-read a conversation and then thought, "Wow! That didn't turn out how I intended"? or "I wish I hadn't said that". We are responsible for our words and we are responsible for knowing when and how to use them. I have learned I can't always go back to fix something, so it is best to make wise choices in the beginning. In doing so, I've experienced less conflict.

Once words leave our mouths, we can't take them back. We can only attempt to explain their context and apologize for the miscommunication. Choose your words wisely.

Part Two- Listening.

Listening to others helps us to learn, to grow and it shows humility. Even if someone's language, dialect, or way of speaking is different from yours, listen with the intent to understand. Oftentimes we get so caught up in formal languages that we nullify what the speaker is saying. And we tend to cut people off ot listen with the intent to respond rather than the intent to understand. Allow them to express themselves and just listen.

Part Three- Respect.

We all have different ways to express ourselves. We have different languages, dialects, tones, vocabulary, and different expressions while speaking. I remember a conversation I had with my son where I was impatient with his storytelling, and I told him to talk faster. He said, *"Actually Mama, I need you to listen slower."* he also told me *"Just because I do not react the way you would does not mean I don't have feelings about it"*. Respecting someone as they are is a show of respect. No one should ever feel like they have to change themselves in order to converse with you. Let people be who they are and let them know who you are. Considering and observing others help us communicate with them on their level.

Words cannot completely communicate what you feel, but the end goal should be to transfer and understand thought, so focus on that with the one whom you are trying to reach.

CHAPTER TWENTY-THREE

Limitations and Boundaries

Excerpt from my diary: *"Today, I got all cute, dropped off the kiddos, drove to work, logged onto my computer, logged off, drove right back home, changed into lounge clothes, opened my curtains and laid down. Nothing "happened," I wasn't "sick," I simply needed a mental health day, so here I lay..."*

Sometimes we can give so much energy to work or people that it will leave you void, drained and unhealthy. I've learned that I am responsible for knowing my limitations and setting my boundaries. Only you know what you are able and willing to give. Giving should come freely and without resentment. Never give so much that you are left at a disadvantage, and never give with the motive of manipulation.

Identify your limitations. Whether it is work, home, family, friends, or leisure, we must recognize our limitations and know what we are able to do. And also know the limitations of others. Some people are able to do much more than what they present and they will never do better as long as they know you will bail them out. Stop giving so much of your time and energy to those people capable of doing for themselves.

Yes, we ought to help one another when we can, but we need to use wisdom when doing so. Some resources are for us to use and some are for us to share. Just because you are able does not mean that you should, and just because you give does not mean you should give without limitations. Set boundaries and you communicate those boundaries. Too much of anything is not a good thing, including too much help.

I gave until I dug myself into a hole. I gave until I was resentful. I gave until it became expected. I gave so much of my mind, that I couldn't think of ways to help myself! I gave so much of my body that

I was tired. I gave so much of my soul that I began to feel hopeless. I gave so much of my time that I had many unfinished projects. Boundaries tell others what, if anything, we are willing to do and it sets limits. I've learned that it is not my duty to fix everyone else's problems. I've learned that there is a difference between helping and enabling. Helping prepares you, enabling does for you.

When I started to say no, my soul said yes! Although others didn't like the fact that I said no, I felt much better. Rather than resentment, I began to feel relief. When I pulled back and empowered others to do for themselves, I felt lighter, more rested, more secure and more at peace. I began to offer guidance rather than an escape. When recognizing my limitations, sometimes I've had to tell myself, *"Even if you want to, No, you cannot."* Or *"It's okay to do that, but here is where you need to stop"*.

Once I started telling people no, some stopped coming around or began interacting with me differently, some got upset and some completely understood. The sincere people still came around, we still talked, they stopped expecting help, and I stopped offering. I began to see their life progress and their confidence build. I could hear their excitement about their accomplishments, and I was so proud of them! Before, I may have looked at them as a burden, but I now look at them with respect!

Learn to say no without guilt and explanation! You do not love people any less because you stop helping them. As a matter of fact, saying no helps people more than it hurts! ***"If there is no struggle, there is no progress." ~ Frederick Douglass.*** This means you need to evaluate a situation and ask yourself, *"Do they need my help or guidance? Are they able to help themselves? How much can I help and how much should I help"?*

Preparing people to help themselves is the best help you can give. Think of the movie "THE WIZ." After an educational, yet frustrating journey, the main character figured out she had what she needed within her all along. Even after repeated attempts to get the Wizard to fix her problem, she was presented a series of challenges and hopes to have her request fulfilled. Along her journey, she established diverse, meaningful relationships, and she had to rely on her own judgment, only to find out, not only was she able to help her friends resolve their problems, but she was quite capable of resolving her own problem all along. And the one who she initially went to for help suffered a lack himself! What an awesome interpretation of growth and maturity!

Practice self-care and make sure your limitations are set by love. There is a reason the captain tells us to put on our life jacket first! "Enough" is an interesting word! It's recognizing you can help, but only so much.

Also, remember that while you are setting and communicating your boundaries, be respectful of the boundaries of others.

In recognizing limitations and setting boundaries, it has restored my faith in men, it has strengthened my confidence in myself, and I still believe in the goodness of people and the beauty of the world.

"I didn't need you to fix me; I needed you to love me while I fixed myself." ~Unknown

CHAPTER TWENTY-FOUR

Responsibility

We must learn to live responsible lives. When we were younger, someone else was responsible for our well being, for deciding what's best for us, deciding what needs to be done and taking the necessary steps to give us the best future. Now that we are adults, we are to be responsible for ourselves. *What exactly is my level of responsibility?*

Our level of responsibility comes at different stages and in different amounts. It's not realistic to compare yours to someone else. For example, by the time I was 17, I had my name on the lease of my own apartment, drove my own car, paid my own bills. I had to get myself up every morning to go to high school, I was responsible for studying and keeping my grades up. Every evening I went to work in a hospital where I was responsible for providing patient care. On the weekends, I worked at a local diner and was responsible for washing dishes.

Not everyone can do these things at this age, however, we must all evaluate the things we are faced with and determine what our level of responsibility really is. Some youth, at a young age, are responsible for contributing financially to the household. Some are responsible for only providing for the things they personally want. Some are responsible for even less.

When my oldest son went off to college, his responsibility was keeping his grades up and his nose clean. As long as he did that, I would give him an allowance and he would not have to work, only focus on school. His responsibility was securing his future. When he finished school and moved back home, his responsibility was helping with house chores, paying his own financial obligations and being respectful of the house and the people in it. Once he passed both of those stages, his responsibility changed to him being responsible for figuring out what he wanted his life to look like and take steps toward establishing himself as independent. He lived with me until he was 22, then left to a place of his own.

Everyone's situation is different, however, you are responsible for doing your part. If I failed to pay my rent, I'd be evicted, if I didn't pay my bills, I'd be disconnected. If I didn't pass my classes, I wouldn't graduate. If I didn't meet expectations at either job, I would have been let go.

We are also responsible for having healthy relationships and setting boundaries with others. Up to a certain point in our lives, certain relationships are defined and established for us but it is up to us to maintain and care for those relationships if we choose to continue them. For example. The family you were born into was not chosen by you. They are the people we are connected with usually from birth (or adoption). You go through many years with these people and you usually have some sort of connection with these people. Once you reach a certain age, those relationships change. The warm and fuzzies towards one another changes. Personalities clash, and sometimes our lives grow in different directions.

Your level of responsibility is determining if and how you will continue the relationship. Now you have to actually put in the work. You have to get to know people on a pure level in order to truly appreciate them. It's easy to adore someone that is caring for your every need. But it gets a little more difficult when you don't need anything from them or if they stop producing, so you are then left deciding how to interact, feel, or think towards them.

One turning point for me was when I was almost 40 years old. I was on the phone with my mother and was crying and upset about something. I was just fussing and ranting about the things I felt I lacked. She listened to me then she calmly said "Tina, I am a person too, have you ever thought about that"? I immediately stopped. I thought wow, I'm good and grown fussing at my mother about something in the past, without respecting the fact that she been finished raising me and is no longer responsible for me so I have no right to speak to her as if she owes me anything. I am responsible for myself.

At some point, we have to realize that our parents are no longer responsible for anything towards us. We have to take up the reigns ourselves and press on. As my dad would say "Load the wagon and shake the line". I changed my tone towards her after that and started talking to her as the woman that gave birth to me and raised me but has a journey of my own to figure out. It's unfair and selfish for me to try and force her to help me carry my load.

So I had to establish a new mindset. Not one that forced submission of my demands, but one that viewed other humans as individuals walking alongside me through this journey. It was then that I was able to recognize that I am responsible for healing my own wounds and paving my own way.

We are responsible for understanding our impact on both our environment and society. Everything that we do impacts not just our lives, but the future generation. We are supposed to leave this place better than we found it, Not leave a mess for someone else to fix. Make conscious choices, considering the impact your actions will have, not only for yourselves but for long-term and environmental effect on our future. Either you are a part of the problem or a part of the solution. We are born to be a part of, not apart from, which means although we are individuals we are still a part of a larger unit and we are responsible for understanding our role.

We are responsible for making the right decisions and making the best use of our time. Even when we make bad decisions, it is our responsibility to learn from them. If we continue to deny and place blame, we aren't learning. We are instead stunting our growth. Learn from it then do better the next time.

None of us have all of the answers, but we are responsible for doing what we can with what we have. Some people had to take advantage of creative opportunities to create something using what they had because failure was not an option for them. No matter how many times they had to try again, their determination gave them the motivation to meet their need.

Responsible people see a need, then take the steps to fill it. Sometimes this even means sacrificing, especially when you get to the point that you are also responsible for others.

CHAPTER TWENTY-FIVE

Accountability

"I say if it's going to be done, let's do it. Let's not put it in the hands of fate, let's not put it in the hands of someone who doesn't know me. I know me best. Then take a deep breath and go ahead".
~Anita Baker

I alone am responsible for my life. It is up to me to determine the vision for my life and work towards it. If I have a lack or if I have a need, it is up to me, first to recognize the lack, identify what resources I need to fill it, then take action to make sure it is filled. Inasmuch, I must also recognize my limitations and know when and whom I need to ask for help.

It is my responsibility to communicate with others. I am responsible for finding the appropriate words to transfer my thoughts. It is my responsibility to listen. Listening gives me information and I am then responsible for deciding how to proceed. If I don't understand something, it is my responsibility to seek clarification. Once I have knowledge it is my responsibility to apply it.

It is up to me to learn how to effectively avoid conflict; however, should a conflict arise, I am responsible for attempting first to resolve the issue, then seeking a mediator if necessary. I also understand I am responsible for myself and cannot force any other individual to do anything against their will.

I am responsible for practicing self-control, making the best decisions, and making adjustments when necessary. I am capable and responsible for my own financial health. Should I have financial difficulties, it is my responsibility to seek financial guidance. In doing so, I understand no one is responsible for repaying my debt but me. I am responsible for taking the steps necessary to become debt-free and to live within my means.

It is my responsibility to develop and maintain healthy relationships. I understand a relationship requires work and compromise. However, I am responsible for healthy communication with others so they can understand me. It is my responsibility to take care of myself and make the best choices for my life. I am responsible for doing, providing, creating, and fixing what is within my power to do. Anything not within my power, I am responsible for seeking resolution. When I am overwhelmed or unable, I am responsible for getting help, or just saying no.

I am responsible for recognizing my limitations. I am responsible for communicating those limitations to others. I am responsible for enforcing my own boundaries. I am responsible for my emotions, my actions and reactions. I am responsible for my feelings, thoughts, and my responses. I am responsible for using my voice. And most importantly, I am responsible for my own happiness.

Responsibility equals accountability. We aren't born with all the answers. We don't always know what to do, but we are responsible for ourselves and our own growth. Your parents and guardians and others can only do so much. After you reach the point of adulthood, you are responsible for taking what you have, recognizing what you lack, and building, fixing, repairing, purging, seeking, and enjoying your life.

CHAPTER TWENTY-SIX

Family

Family is our foundation, the first people we form relationships with, the first people we interact daily with, those we grow with, love, support, and usually have some level of understanding with. A healthy family is integral in laying foundations, teaching principles and culture, cultivating growth and giving us the tools we need to begin our journey to a successful life. Our Family will always be a part of us, but *what role does family play in our adult lives?*

In most families, once you're an adult, the family has done its primary job of raising and grooming you. They are no longer responsible for providing dependent care for you. It's now time to establish yourself and to begin caring for your needs.

Sometimes we get so comfortable at home that we fail to establish independence. Family isn't meant to coddle and hold us forever. Remaining in a dependent state can limit us, causing complacency and stagnation. Independence, however, builds confidence, character, and identity. When I lived at home, I cooked like my mother, stored toiletries like my mother, and I was financially immature. When I had a place of my own, I learned new recipes, decided I liked different toiletries, wanted them to be stored differently, and I learned to budget. It's not to say there's something wrong with the way my parents did things, but I learned a new way of doing things in my own environment.

When you remain at home, you have confidence in the people you live with, that they will continue to care for and make choices and provisions for you. When you establish your own, you have confidence in yourself, your ability and your choices.

If the only people we attach ourselves to are the ones we were born and raised with, the ones that we depend on, then we rob ourselves of the opportunity to establish genuine relationships with others. Our family should prepare us to blaze our own path, and staying under the constant protection of them is disallowing yourself to spread your wings and fly. It also denies you the opportunity to learn to trust God for yourself and develop your own sense of confidence.

Understandably, not everyone comes from a nurturing, loving home. So sometimes you have to leave behind the things of your youth. This is when you let any dysfunctional family teachings, habits, thoughts and traditions go. If you were raised under certain unhealthy circumstances, it is up to you if you whether or not to continue that path. Patterns and traditions run deep, so you discover what helps you grow and build off that. Likewise, discover which patterns or teachings damaged you and change them.

You are an adult now, and it is your responsibility to figure out how to run your own life. If you recognize unhealthy teaching and continue that way as an adult, then it is no longer your family to blame for holding you back. Rise up!

This is also true of the family who does not want to let you grow. You have to set boundaries and you have to learn to say no. Many times we make decisions for our lives based off of our family's desires and requests, then end up causing resentment, conflict or stagnation. Familial obligations can change the course of our lives so we must learn to set limitations and communicate our boundaries. Sometimes you have to be emotionally blind so you won't be emotionally blackmailed. In other words, if this person was not related to you and gave such demands, would it affect your decisions?

Once you leave the comfort of the home created for you, from familiar people and surroundings, you can focus on establishing a life of your own and forming healthy relationships with others. Family is not to be disregarded, in fact, family can be a wonderful resource of love and support. After all, they are a part of who we are, but just because someone is family, does not give them the right to dictate your life.

Believe in yourself! Once you take steps to establish

independence, don't leave with the mindset that you'll voluntarily return to safety. And don't completely shut family out. Leave knowing, should you really need safety, your family will be a resource, but it is your responsibility to try your best to establish a life for yourself. Then get to know your family on a different level. Respect your foundation, while building your future.

Martina Alford

CHAPTER TWENTY-SEVEN

Friends

Excerpts from my diary: *"Do you feel like I can't handle you or do you feel like I am just not worthy to know you?"* ~Martina

Having close relationships with people who we are not related to, is a healthy way to network, build confidence, and strengthen our perception of reality. Friends are strangers we choose to get to know and be a part of our lives. When with friends we should feel comfortable enough to be ourselves, to get to know them, and allow them to get to know us. It is wise to build friendships, but it takes work. True friendship is built over time, strengthened through trials, improved through honesty and anchored in honor and respect. Friends help mold each other while being molded.

Many of us have childhood friends who we grew up with, played with, and hung around. Childhood friends gave us some of our best lessons about having fun, resolving conflict, taking risks, speaking our mind and most of all, forgiveness. As a child, conflict is usually resolved quickly and either you were soon playing again or decided to just steer clear from each other. At that age, you usually choose friends you are surrounded by the most and who you played well with. In adolescence, you begin to choose friends you have more in common with, can relate to and feel good to be around. This is also the age children form cliques. They begin choosing friends who they can identify with. Then in adulthood, you learn to choose friends who are like-minded, mutual in investment, have something in common, are on the same page and have the same vibe.

The friends we choose can make a great impact on our lives, our choices, and the person we become. Some friends grow with us, and the relationship gets stronger, while other friends are seasonal and the relationship eventually ends. When you are selective about your friends, you know who they are, what they have to offer, how they affect you and likewise you with them. It's a two-way street, in which you both should benefit.

I've had a friend for over twenty years who pushes me and challenges me to do better and be better. He calls me out when I'm not being my truest self and challenges my thoughts, actions, and even my reactions. Although we have distinctly different personalities, we are both very passionate people, and our friendship balances one another. When we disagree, it's not with the intent to clone thought but rather to evoke understanding. In other words, you do not have to agree with your friend in order to understand where they are coming from; you just have to respect their perspective. Yes, our personality differences sometimes cause conflict, but our friendship is more valuable than a disagreement, so we always find a way to a respectful end.

We haven't always been this way. There were periods of time where we went days, weeks, months and even a few years with hurt feelings and without speaking, but we always managed to close the gap. We had to learn to value one another, learn to communicate, respect each other's feelings and differences. We've had to learn patience and consideration. Now, we talk freely, listen more, and have learned how to disagree. We've also learned limitations, when to pull back and when to give each other space. If your friends don't challenge you to be a better person, live up to your full potential and just be naturally you, then you need to re-evaluate them.

Friendship is an investment. You have to be willing to give just as much as you are expecting. Get to know your friend, their history, likes, dislikes, dreams, goals, their personality, and preferences. Get to know their perspectives, find out their triggers, and allow them to get to know the same about you. Your friend should be able to rely on you when needed and vice versa.

Another friend told me, "*You actually made me a better player. You used to kick my butt constantly when I first started playing. I loved the competition!*" Being your best can cause someone else to strive for their best! You never know who is watching and needing you. I have a dear, sweet friend who is as peaceful, kind, and considerate as can be. She smiles a lot and gives the best hugs! There's a lot about her I admire and we can talk for hours about the dynamics of womanhood! She keeps me from becoming cynical. We don't always have to say or do everything right; we just have to be honest. If they love everything you say and do, then the odds are good they aren't being true.

Hold on to great friends but allow your circle to grow. Not everyone will have the same level of friendship, but it is wise to have more than one friend. Friendship shouldn't be heavy, binding, stressful or troublesome. As long as we live, we will continue to evolve, but the core of true friendship will remain even as we all inevitably change.

The keys to a wonderful friendship are communication, honesty, spending quality time getting to know one another, giving your support and learning how to juggle your time.

CHAPTER TWENTY-EIGHT

Pride

Excerpt from my diary: *"She tried to warn me. She tried to tell me to wait. But I didn't listen. And now, here I am upset and crying from something preventable. I have to admit, I kept going because I didn't see. I didn't understand. I did not look beyond myself. I was too prideful to consider she just may be able to see something I cannot. I did not give her credit. I did not listen to her guidance. My pride got in the way, and now I'm paying the price."*

Pride is a very strong thing with has a huge impact on our lives. It both positively and negatively affects who we are and how we handle our life. It either hold us up to a high standard, or it takes us down a path of stubbornness, roadblocks, and hindrances.

Negative pride is filled with stubbornness and ego. It causes you to be inconsiderate and self-centered. It can stop you from establishing sincere relationships, providing clear communication and from building on a solid foundation. Negative pride makes you believe you have all the answers. It prevents you from listening to the wisdom of others. It causes you to make decisions contrary to warnings because you would rather do what you want. It makes you think your way is the only way to do things and your opinions are the only ones that matter. Pride makes you believe you don't need anyone and you can do everything alone. It tells you that you'd rather struggle than to ask for help. Pride makes you blame others for your mistakes and never accepting responsibility for your own choices.

Pride can also be a good thing. When you are pleased with yourself, choices you've made and what you've accomplished, it builds confidence, gives you a sense of belonging, and helps build a sense of value for your life. It is perfectly fine to be proud of yourself, where you come from, and where you are headed when you make progressive steps toward your goals.

As a matter of fact, setting a high standard for life and holding yourself to it, gives you a sense of value, dignity, and shows self-control. When you hold yourself accountable for the decisions you've made, it shows humility and self-respect. Take pride in the standards you set. Don't accept less than what is right for you. Be proud of your vision for your life, and give your best effort in all you do.

Even when you make mistakes, you should be proud, not of the mistake itself, but in the acknowledging the results of your choice. Be proud that you are responsible enough to make choices for yourself. When you take pride in your choices, you usually have a positive outcome, because you've taken your future into consideration. When you set goals or have assigned tasks you've fulfilled, you should be proud of your accomplishments. It motivates you to not only finish but in the best way possible.

Be proud of your history. When you are proud of where you come from, you can appreciate how far you've come. Being proud of your roots is important because, although no family is perfect, the place you came from and the things you've been through have placed you on the journey to become who you are today. The more I learn about my history, the more I understand about myself.

Sometimes we would like to run from and forget some things we've experienced, but until we acknowledge them and how they affect us today, we will be missing a piece of who we are. Being proud of your past does not mean you desire to mimic or stay there, it simply puts you in a mindset of understanding yourself, to see how far you've come. Be proud of even the dark times. Once you come out, you can see just how strong you are, and you you'll have a testimony.

Pride is holding onto your standards, it is the influence of your decisions, and it is that feeling of happiness when you know you've done well. Pride is not only accomplishing something but also doing your very best at it.

Although I see room for improvement, I am very proud of who

I am right now. I am proud of the things I have overcome, accomplished, and the life I have created for myself. I've learned from my mistakes. I see the things I have avoided. I see the perseverance. I see growth.

Excerpts from my diary: *"As I stood, staring in the mirror, I had to ask myself, "What is it I do not see?"*

Don't ever be so prideful that you refuse to acknowledge yourself or learn from others. Be proud of yourself, but not prideful. Be confident but not arrogant. Humility is your friend.

CHAPTER TWENTY-NINE

Society and Acceptance

Excerpts from my diary: *"Are you perfect yet?"*

How much influence does our environment and the people around us have on us? How much are we changed or controlled by what we see?

We live in a world full of temptation, where the goal is to make us feel we are lacking something, so we seek to fulfill what we think we need. Temptations are presented to make you think more value will be added to your life by obtaining those things.

We've become hungry for constant stimulation, so much so, that if we are not entertained constantly or on demand, we often use words like boring and basic, to describe any other circumstance. We tend to gravitate towards people, places, and things to immediately fill our need for stimulation, yet we tend to have a limited attention span before moving to the next source of entertainment. We live in a very "entertain me" society. Either you are the one demanding constant stimulation, or you're being pressured to capture and retain someone else's attention.

We constantly compare ourselves to others. Oh, the pressure to match or surpass what someone else has, who they are dating, where they live, what they know, who they know, where they work, how they look, and the list goes on and on. We over involve ourselves in the lives of others, wondering and watching their next move, then planning to make ours. We even compare our level of happiness to theirs. We give in to trends; our esteem is based on popularity, we desire acceptance and are swayed by opinions. These are all held in high regard and treated as the rite of passage for our lives.

Why are we so obsessed with acceptance? Why do we constantly seek perfection, and who have we empowered to set those standards?

We live in a world where there's an unattainable perfection checklist, and we obsess with which box we can mark. Many of us are in constant competition with others to check as many boxes as possible. #Goals

We obsess over physical appearance. Did you know, regardless of your DNA, your body, especially your face, is genuinely sculpted by your atmosphere and your personality? The facial expressions that make you unique are the ones that exercise the muscles and tone your face. The more you exercise those muscles, the more specific your face gets. For example, a smile and frown each use different muscles, therefore, naturally your cheeks and brow lines are affected. A surgeon may be able to create a visualization based upon your desired description, however, they cannot duplicate facial personality.

We also obsess over our skin color and texture. We want the facial wrinkles gone but neglect to acknowledge the natural progression of aging. We cover up with makeup and potions because we want blemish free, smooth, hairless skin. We fixate over hair, to the point we cover it up, regulate and even have laws passed mandating how it can be worn! Our obsession has lead us to ignore the fact that many have lost their hair or can't grow any at all. Yet we accept the illusion of "approved" hair. Then there's the eyebrow obsession. Two patches of hair stuck near the top of our face, and we are consumed with perfecting them. We obsess over height, weight, and body shape. The things we negatively obsess about, others oftentimes view differently.

We obsess over the way we talk and the language we use, all while failing to acknowledge every person's tongue is different. Everyone's brain process things differently. The way we hear, understand, and repeat sounds are different. We obsess over the job we choose, oftentimes choosing a job of status rather than a profession of fulfillment. We reach for name brands or flashy items, then worry about protecting them so no one can steal from us.

We obsess over the name we are given. Our name is the individual title we are given at birth. The compilation of letters and sounds we answer to when we recognize someone is addressing us specifically. We don't care about edibles called Kumquats or Cucumbers, Pickles or Turmeric. We don't care if you call it a sedan or a limousine, a bike or a rollerblade. All of these are funny sounding words we accept, but we obsess over a person's name.

We focus on where we were raised and where we were educated, as if we had a choice and as if it makes us more or less important in comparison to someone raised and educated elsewhere. We obsess over what kind of car we drive, what garments we choose, and what type of devices we have.

My question is, after you've checked off your list of perfection when you close your eyes, when you feel your breath, when you lay awake, are you happy? Are you perfect? Are you accepted? Does society applaud you? Do you fit in? Do they know your name? Have you made your mark? Are you important now?

The things we see around us are images of the lives other people have created for themselves. Everything is not for everyone, and we should not try to mimic others. Don't get caught up in the illusion of how things appear. When we live a life defined by others, we will live a life unfulfilled. People change, standards change, and trends change. If you continue to be defined by the standards of social norms, you will constantly change too.

You are incomparable to everyone else. If someone knows you, they should be able to distinctly explain who you are, rather than you blending in as just another clone lost in the crowd. Be a trendsetter, make your own way, create your own path, and own your uniqueness. What's more important to you? Acceptance of others or acceptance of yourself? Rather than living up to the illusion of society's perfect standards, you should set your own! Start your own trend, make your own wave, and make them remember your name! Be who you were created to be. The world has plenty of people, but there's only one you.

CHAPTER THIRTY

Environment

Excerpts from my diary: *"Our home is a place of peace. The only thing that we fight is against anything that threatens that."* ~*Martina*

In order to impact the world, you must first impact your neighborhood. In order to impact your neighborhood, you must impact your block. In order to impact your block, you must impact your home. In order to impact your home, you must first master yourself.

Not everyone has had a healthy representation of home, therefore, some people only know how to mimic what they were surrounded by. When we come from an unhealthy situation, we absorb that environment, then as adults, we tend to recreate dysfunction in our own lives.

Some of us were raised in a dysfunctional home and weren't even aware. We grew so accustomed to what we saw that we didn't question abnormalities. As a matter of fact, sometimes we get so caught up that we tend to look at life through a pessimistic lens and view any other way of life as an unattainable fairy tale. And then there are the people who were fortunate enough to have grown up in a wonderfully prepared home with love overflowing, abundance, safety, structure, and hope. A peaceful place that's warm and welcoming and makes you glow at the thought of it. The place we long for when we are away.

We are all different, raised differently and see things differently. Don't assume everyone was raised the same way or have the same level of understanding as you. A friend once told me, *"Make sure you find out how people were raised. Some were raised off survival, not love"*. No home is perfect, however, we can't expect the next generation to be anything other than a modern version of what we expose them to, and in doing so, we can't blame them. You now carry the burden of breaking the chains that bind you or you will likely affect your children.

Regardless of how you were raised, you have to decide what kind of life you will create for yourself. You can live in a mansion filled with despair or a shack filled with love. Regardless of the size, appearance, and contents of a house, home is an atmosphere that goes with you wherever you go. A healthy home is a place steady and strong. When you have a healthy home, you have the comfort and support to make it through. Sure, we can get attached to a physical location with some furniture, the layout, and the address, but the physical structure does not make a home. Home is a place within.

In order to have a peaceful home, decide what life you want and what it looks like. Anything a part of your home, happening in your home or allowed in your home that you no longer want to be a part of, take steps to remove it. Anything causing stress, makes you feel down or stagnant, remove it. Sometimes removing things simply means saying no or no more. Next, you must decide what it is you do want. You have the power to add anything to your home that fits your vision. I knew I wanted peace, love, comfort, a place free to communicate without judgment, a place where you are encouraged to be yourself, love, support and the ability to grow.

Once you create the life you want, protect it. Your home is your haven, your safe place, and anyone or anything threatening peace in your home must be addressed so your home can return to a place of tranquility.

CHAPTER THIRTY-ONE

Decisions

"One of the things I think young people, especially nowadays, should learn is how to see for yourself and listen for yourself and think for yourself. Then you can come to an intelligent decision for yourself. "~Malcom X.

We are responsible for making decisions about our own lives. From the smallest events like what to eat for your meals, to large events like where you will live, require a decision. Making good decisions require thought and consideration. Think about what outcome you expect, and identify your options. Think about the pros and cons, and then make the best decision with the information you have.

Avoid allowing others to make or influence your decisions. Yes, it is wise to seek guidance when necessary and consider their advice, but the final decision should be yours. Once you make a decision, evaluate the results, and then own it. Even if something doesn't turn out as planned, learn from it. Understand there is a difference between a mistake and a bad decision. A mistake is when you make a choice that unintentionally turns out bad, like being in the wrong place at the wrong time. You did not intend for anything bad to happen, but you were there when it did. A bad decision is having all of the information and making a decision anyway without regarding the consequence. In other words, you know it may not turn out good, but you decided to do it anyway.

Good decisions don't always guarantee the outcome you want, and bad decisions don't condemn you. When we have a negative outcome, we can learn from our experience in hopes to never repeat it again. Not all decisions can be avoided. In this life, there are some lessons you just have to learn. The choices we make either give us confidence or teach us a lesson. We have to live with the consequences of our decisions, and yes, some consequences follow us our whole lives, so choose wisely! We always have a choice even if it's not the ones we want.

"Your true self is who you are when you remove all emotions and fear from your choices." ~Martina

CHAPTER THIRTY-TWO

Perseverance

Excerpts from my diary: *"I called my aunt today with tears falling down my face, ranting about how hard my life is and how things are not working out. How I just want to give up and how blah blah blah... She listened to me get it all off my chest, then said, "Girl, you are throwing a pity party and don't nobody want to come." I then dried up my tears, fixed my face and went downstairs to make dinner."*

Sometimes, after you've ranted, cried, complained and regrouped, you just have to push through! Ok yes, we may have many reasons why we are frustrated, have not progressed or why we are in a bad situation, but we are still alive and must still press on.

So you've had a tough life. People hurt and abandoned you? Are things not working out for you? How long are you going to lay there day after day telling people your story of getting walked on, picked over, stories of your ailment and your torment? How much do you desire to be greater? At some point, we have to stop talking about our roadblocks and just get up and do better!!

Sometimes we are so busy remembering what stops us, that we don't see other doors wide open. We must take every opportunity to advance. Do you know that your limitation is only a small factor in the big picture? You have to find creative ways to keep your mind and spirit alive while enduring trials.

Your limitations may slow you down, but they shouldn't stop you. Use those as tools to take you to the next level. At each level, there are a different set of circumstances, obstacles, and rewards, but you have to make it there in order to see what's next. Yes, things may be difficult now, but I would rather push through hard work to get to the next level, rather than staying in a difficult situation. It's not just a matter of setting a goal, but life is in the details. Your journey is just as important as the destination.

Make people remember your name. Make them say, "Oh my! She's at it again!" Make your mark! I remember going for an interview in the field of my degree. I was a top candidate but didn't get the job. I was told that it was between me and another interviewee, who got the job because he had more experience. I was told, "*We really want you.*" and I was given advice on what to do, so I took the advice. About a year later another position on the same team came open, and I reapplied. The same supervisor interviewed me and smiled! "*I remember you from the last time! You did as we recommended! You have the job.*" That's Perseverance! Not giving up even if the odds are against you!

There have been many times I just wanted to give up. I'm not always strong, the road is not always easy and there will always be some kind of difficulty, but no matter how much I cry, no matter how much I whine or get frustrated, my will to do well is always stronger. I will bend, but I won't break. So I rise!

No matter how long you live you will never "finish." There will always be something else you'll have to face. You may finish one task or another, but as the old saying goes, "*It ain't over until it's over.*" Don't think too much about what you are doing. Sometimes you just gotta do. Get up and make the best of today!

CHAPTER THIRTY-THREE

Time

I wrote this chapter on the day that someone close to me died. I got a phone call that morning saying he was in the hospital and "it doesn't look good". I said what do you mean? I stood there shocked and trying to decipher what exactly "not good" meant. No sooner than I got back to my desk came the second phone call "he's gone".

Time is most humanly identified as the period of our existence. We attempt to explain it by using words equivalent to certain increments, but honestly, time cannot really be counted nor contained. There is no identifiable beginning nor end. Time just is!

The way we identify time is not the same way time actually exists. Can you tell me the moment life began and when does it end? When does the sun reaches its highest peak, or when does the season actually change? When does the leaf turn green? When do our nails grow? Does the clock change after the second or on the second? Are seconds counted by the onset of time itself or according to the identified period of time by the first clockmaker? Did our conversation begin when I spoke the words or when you heard them?

You see what I mean? You can't really define time, can you? Time is and was and will continue to be. Time cannot truly be counted only lived. Even when the period of time we capture has expired, time itself will continue. Time is an irreplaceable gift. Of all the things life has to offer, time is the one thing that cannot be bought yet holds the most value. How you choose to spend it is up to you. When things are bought, places are visited, and dreams accomplished, the only thing left is the memory of the way we lived our assigned time. How will you spend yours?

We have to develop a lifestyle which allows us to live fully with the amount of time we are given. I have learned to slow down. Sometimes we rush through life so fast that we miss precious moments. I realized I was rushing through life in an effort to get things done, and I didn't give sufficient time to what and who was in front of me.

Once it is spent, it's gone. I've noticed that I always feel better when I spend time rather than money. Whether it's a little rest, a kiss, a hug, a break, a smile or a breath between storms, if it's a compliment, a warm hello, or a conversation with someone I know, I may not always remember the item you bought me, but I will always remember the time you shared!

You won't master life in one day, one week, one year, or some predefined increment. Breathe, relax, enjoy and grow as you go!

CHAPTER THIRTY-FOUR

Just Like That

'tis better to have loved and lost than never to have loved at all
~ Alfred Lord Tennyson.

All of this has been surreal. I was almost finished writing this book. The cover was finalized and approved, the contents were reviewed and I was ready to upload! Then just like that, I have another chapter to write.

I had just gotten off the phone with my dad. He told me that he was in the hospital and ate french toast, sausage, and eggs for breakfast (but he didn't care for the eggs too much). I told him I was going to come to see him but he said: "just wait, It's no big deal, okay". Daddy was never sick besides the common cold. He never complained, he was never down. He was strong and sensible and steadfast, so this hospital talk was something new.

I promised to call back and check on him around the clock and told him to go ahead and file those retirement papers and he is coming to live with me in Tennessee. "You would do that for me?" Daddy asked. "Yes Dad, I will. Get better soon so you can come". When we got off the phone I sent my dad a text: "Daddy! My cover is finished! The text is finally approved and my book is finally ready for print!". He didn't reply.

Little did I know, his condition had progressed. We made it to his bedside the next day. The next couple weeks were spent basically camping out at the hospital by his side, up until the moment that I stood there, with my hands over his heart and felt his heart beat for the very last time. I cannot believe this!

Gone is the man that I talk to every day. Gone is the man that knows all about me but loves me anyway. Gone is the man that tells me the truth as God sees it, not swayed by opinions. Gone is the one consistent man in my life. The one that taught me how to do stuff, how to focus, the one that accepted all my broken pieces and constantly told me how proud he was of me and how amazed he is at me. He got so excited when he learned new things about me. He always had words of reality and encouragement and was my biggest supporter! Gone is the man whose words continue to guide me. He's gone! And I can't believe it!

The days following his passing was a whirlwind of arrangements and decisions, much of it a blur. This is when the support of family and friends helped a lot. This is when our faith was tested and we had to trust our decisions. This is when I was faced with the validity of every single chapter in this book.

Once the day came that all this was over, no more phone calls, no more hospital, no more funeral home, it was back on the road to go back home. Then it hit me. As I walked into my house, I dropped my bags, and stood in the middle of my room and cried. "What do I do now? I'm supposed to just unpack my bags and figure out a new life without dad?".

The answer is Yes.

I have his features, his hands, his feet, his caring nature for others and his contagious smile! We thing similarly. Have similar sense of humor. I hear him every day and I feel him every day. I miss my dad so much! He's been a huge part of my life. I still grab my phone in the mornings looking for his text, only…. I have his phone… And it is now disconnected.

I am so grateful for the time God allowed dad to be on earth with us. I am grateful for the hard years, the misunderstandings, the laughter, and the tears. I'm grateful for my relationship with him. It was unconditional, tried and true. I am grateful for the "good years" we had. I am grateful we were there to share his transition from this place. I'm grateful to have felt his last heartbeat.

So now losing Daddy is a part of my Mosaic. This is real. My life forever changed. I'm going to figure it out, daddy. I'm going to make you even more proud. My life must reflect the very best of everything because that's all he ever wanted. I'll figure out how.

"Don't worry about the mule being blind, just load the wagon and shake the line." That's my favorite quote from daddy. He would always tell me not to focus so much on adversity, just do my part.

Although he never replied, I later found out that the last thing dad did after we talked, the morning of Saturday, July 28, 2018, at 10:50 AM, from his hospital room, was save a snapshot of this book cover into the gallery of his phone. Then two weeks later on Saturday, August 11, 2018, at 9:40 PM, exactly 45 years to the day that he married our mother, I felt his last heartbeat, and just like that, my Dad's passing is now an eternal piece of my Mosaic.

My life is not my own. There's more to come…

THE END

M.O.S.A.I.C

Taking all the pieces of your life and creating a masterpiece.

Mosaic is a masterpiece created by taking many pieces and purposely arranging them into an artistic expression. I want to encourage you today to take all of the pieces of your life and put them in place to create something beautiful!

Motivation

Observation

Self-control

Accountability

Intuition

Choice

In everything we are, everything we do, everything we know, and everything we encounter, we must take all of it, and we have to purposely create something so it can work for our good.

I encourage and challenge you to recognize the power you already have so you can be the best version of yourself. You have to put in the work and trust God to do the rest.

We are all still a work in progress! There is always another piece to add! Faith is the glue!

ABOUT THE AUTHOR

Martina A. Alford was born and raised in East Saint Louis, Illinois, in 1976, to Gwendolyn (Ewing) Alford and Donald L. Alford Sr., with her older brother and three younger siblings.

She graduated from a vocational high school where she earned her Nursing Aide Certification which allowed her to work a short time in patient care. She relocated to Atlanta, Georgia in 1995 and enrolled in an Electronics and Computer Technology program where she earned an Associates of Applied Science Degree from DeVry Institute of Technology. She later moved to Chattanooga, Tennessee in 2002, and began to work in the Information Technology field.

While in Chattanooga, Martina began motivational speaking, while honing her skills as a Spoken Word artist, Blogger, Encourager, and super planner.

Martina started a Mommy and Me group which was designed to cultivate relationships between mothers and their daughters and to foster connections between mothers. She is passionate about healthy families and believes in bridging the gap between raising children and building strong, meaningful relationships with them.

Martina is a mother to three children: Sons, Chauncey (graphic designer), Amon (an aspiring chef), and daughter, Tarina (who sews and custom makes garments and became an entrepreneur of a handmade accessory line starting at the age of 7).

Martina believes that the wisdom we acquire through our lives should not be held on to merely for the purpose of storytelling but should be used as a foundation to help build and guide the next generation. Although some things must be learned on one's own, some things can be shared with others to help pave a little understanding along their journey.

Martina presently resides in Chattanooga, Tennessee.

To contact Martina Alford:

Website: https://ionlyknowonesong.com

E-mail: IOnlyKnowOneSong@gmail.com

Twitter: MOSAIC by Martina Alford

Instagram: Mosaic_by_martina_alford

Facebook: One Song

Thank You,
Martina Alford

www.ingramcontent.com/pod-product-compliance
Lightning Source LLC
Chambersburg PA
CBHW020917090426
42736CB00008B/670